OUT OF TUNE

Listening to the First Amendment

John Frohnmayer

NORTH AMERICAN PRESS
a division of Fulcrum Publishing
Golden, Colorado
1995

The author is indebted to the
Freedom Forum First Amendment Center
at Vanderbilt University where much of this book was written.

Copyright © 1995 John Frohnmayer

First published by The Freedom Forum First Amendment Center at Vanderbilt University, © September 1994.
Publication No. 94-F07

The author is grateful for permission to quote from the following works:

"To a Commencement of Scoundrels," by Samuel Hazo. From *Thank A Bored Angel,* © 1983. Used with permission of the author.

"Letter from Birmingham Jail," by Martin Luther King, Jr. Reprinted by arrangement with The Heirs to the Estate of Martin Luther King, Jr., c/o Joan Daves Agency as agent for the proprietor. Copyright © 1963, 1964 by Martin Luther King, Jr., copyright renewed 1991, 1992 by Coretta Scott King.

Library of Congress Cataloging-in-Publication Data

Frohnmayer, John.
      Out of tune : listening to the First Amendment / John Frohnmayer.
         p.   cm.
      First work originally published: Freedom Forum First Amendment Center at Vanderbilt University, 1994.
      Includes bibliographical references and index.
      ISBN 1-55591-932-4
        1. United States—Constitution—Amendments—1st. 2. Freedom of speech—United States. 3. Censorship—United States. I. Titles.
KF4770.F78   1995
342.73'0853—dc20   95-12267
[347.302853]   CIP

Book Design by Pat Staten • Cover Design by William Spahr
Cover photograph by Jennifer Berman, copyright © 1995

Printed in the United States of America

North American Press
A division of Fulcrum Publishing
350 Indiana Street, Suite 350, Golden, Colorado 80401-5093 USA
800/992-2908

CONTENTS

Introduction   vii

Chapter 1   Politics   1

Chapter 2   Ethics   20

Chapter 3   Censorship and Its Progeny   34

Chapter 4   Religion and Government   53

Chapter 5   Our Troubled History of Reunion   66

Epilogue   77

Appendix I: The Declaration of Independence   80

Appendix II: The Constitution of the United States   87

Appendix III: The Gettysburg Address   113

Appendix IV: Letter from Birmingham Jail   115

Index   133

INTRODUCTION

Liberty means responsibility, that's why most men dread it.
—George Bernard Shaw

OUR THIRST FOR OUTRAGE has become a national obsession. We are assaulted repeatedly by examples of fathers abandoning their children, businesses duping customers, politicians betraying their trust. Daily radio and television fare consists of people publicly discussing their most private affairs or complaining nonstop about a society out of control. Four-letter words substitute for meaningful discussion, and exaggerated presentations scream through our shields of self-protection. The First Amendment is to blame. Its forty-five ordinary words grant us license to communicate, even when the subject matter is disgusting, degrading or useless.

Would the First Amendment pass a popular vote today? Polls tell us it might not, because while each of us wants to protect our own religion, we're not sure about the other person, and we are annoyed by hate speech, or partisan speech, or lewd and insulting speech, or violence on television. And yet, we watch it. We clamor for more at the same time we denounce those who give it to us.

Paradoxically, while we wallow in outrage, we are so concerned with not giving offense in racial, gender, and religious issues that we are polite to the point of impotence. We have developed a kind of social kabuki that prevents us from having to deal with these serious issues. We talk in code, double-talk, and qualifiers, and as a result, we have lost—or are losing—the common basis of agreement and understanding that we call the social contract.

And we have lost our nerve. Free speech and open debate are risky. Excessive television violence and gutter language are examples of that risk. This book, however, is based upon an affirmation fundamental to the American soul—an affirmation of optimism about our future and our ability to achieve our own goals. America has a self-help obsession, whether it be for diet, fitness, sexual fulfillment or spiritual peace. The premise discussed in this book is that the pursuit of happiness evoked in the Declaration of Independence is not one free of pain, struggle, frustration, mistake or failure. But in that pursuit is the exhilarating, compelling, and fulfilling belief that we are in charge of our lives, that we are free to make our own choices, and that our faith can be directed as we choose. Fulfillment is found in hard work and personal responsibility and, yes, in sacrifice. The goal is not just individual fulfillment, but the common good. The government is our hotel. We own it. We aren't guests to be pampered.

When we are outraged, we are disconnected; we are not participants. When there is no penalty for falsehood, be it in politics or social life, we are disconnected. We demand no accountability. This book is about rediscovering our fundamental principles and the responsibilities inherent in them. These documents—the Declaration of Independence, Constitution and the Bill of Rights—are our fundamental ethical and legal foundations. They offer us a chance to analyze our numerous shortcomings and rededicate ourselves to do better. If we don't check out.

Writer and poet, Maya Angelou, talks about our having been "paid for" by the struggles of our ancestors. It is this credo of steward-ship, of power, and of self-definition that will help refocus our American values. Here is how she states the challenge: "Are we not the same people who worked, prayed, planned and dreamed of a country where the idea of freedom was in the national conscience, and dignity was a part of the national framework?"

Values. This is a word that's precariously close to "value"—get-ting our money's worth. What this book is about is *giving* value rather than getting it. The paradox is that the more value we give, either in the ethical sense of protecting others' right to express or hold ideas, or in the political sense of setting common goals and then respecting those who have a different vision of how to get there, the more value we receive. If we are totally engaged, we realize that we are, in fact, pursuing happiness with our lives and our liberty.

The return to the first principles described in these chapters is likely to cost everyone something. The vast middle of the political spectrum will lose complacency; the right wing some outrage; the left wing some righteous guilt; young people some disengaged cool. All of us will suffer some postponement of gratification. Our journey back toward our first principles will take tiny steps toward a common goal of a society that more closely matches our founding ideas than what we presently have. It is a journey toward the dream that Martin Luther King, Jr. articulated in his 1963 March on Washington speech. The liberty we are pursuing here is both an ideal and a process. It's an ideal because, as we shall see, freedom, equality, protection of and from religion are goals which, throughout our history, we have nei-ther achieved completely nor completely abandoned. And it is a pro-cess, because it requires involvement of its citizens (and that means you). So here's a preview of the text you hold in your hand, an outline of the shape of this book, to be filled in by your participation.

The first chapter presents the Declaration of Independence as the fundamental moral document of the United States, just as the

Constitution is the fundamental legal document. Together these two form a foundation anchored by freedom at one end and responsibility at the other. Politics has some rules, and this book suggests a few— such as truth-telling—but the important rules are the ones which we discover, and then, throughout our lives, demand that those who work for us—our politicians—follow.

The second chapter is on ethics. If politics is the art of the possible, ethics keeps us on course by establishing ideals toward which we can strive. Politics without ethics is a ship without a rudder. Our ethical conscience allows us to criticize our sometimes puny efforts at self-determination.

In the third chapter, we consider what would happen if we didn't have free speech. Censorship, a universal impulse from the beginning of history, denies some people access to writings or images or sounds or ideas. An artwork utilizing the American flag is the focal point for this discussion.

We turn to religion, and particularly to prayer in public schools, in the fourth chapter. Is a student-led, student-initiated minute of silence consistent with the First Amendment and our pledge of liberty and equality for all? Is the route to better behavior and a more civil society the establishment of prayer in public institutions? Let's analyze it.

Finally, just as Abraham Lincoln looked back to the Declaration of Independence as the foundation for his Gettysburg Address, so Martin Luther King, Jr. also sought its inspiration for his "Letter from Birmingham Jail." We will study those documents in the fifth chapter, and then, perhaps, you can draft an address that articulates your own stake in democracy.

This book is not meant to eliminate controversy. It is meant to focus it. At the end of each chapter are questions for discussion and a recommended reading list. Debate and confrontation are the mother's milk of democracy. We can use them constructively.

Chapter One

POLITICS

I will act as if what I do makes a difference.
—William James

You have the right to free speech.
As long as you're not dumb enough to actually try it.
—The Clash, "Know Your Rights"
from *Combat Rock*

SO WHICH IS IT? Are we pawns of a heartless political machine or masters of our own destiny? Do we have rights of speech and meaningful participation in our government, or are those blessings claimed only by the few, the white, the rich, the fortuitously born? Do we agree that our fate is one fate—both as a nation and a society—or shall we go it alone, thinking that what we get must be at the expense of someone else? The question is addressed by our founding documents, and the answer is there, too.

The Declaration of Independence

Understanding American politics means understanding the Declaration of Independence and the Constitution, particularly the First Amendment. Zealots, not accommodators, wrote these documents. They proved that the stock of human wisdom has been increased not by those who have agreed, but by those who have challenged the established order. It was their willingness to think broadly, to encounter the headwind of change and, above all, to take risks that established our rights and freedoms. We must be as courageous and as dedicated to keep them.

The Declaration of Independence is made up of three parts. The first is the philosophical justification for freedom, the second a list of complaints against King George III, and the last a declaration of separation from the British Crown. While it invokes "The Laws of Nature and of Nature's God" for its authority, it argues to men, seeking approval in "the court of world opinion." It affirms that men are endowed "by their Creator with unalienable rights, which no government can take away." It appeals "to the Supreme Judge of the World" to bless the moral rightness of freedom from tyranny. Regardless of whether this appeal is to the Judeo-Christian God, the deistic God, or simply to a Benign Presence, the philosophical justification for the colonies' action is rationality—the Enlightenment Rule of Reason flowing from the thoughts of René Descartes, John Locke and, arguably the American cleric, Roger Williams.

Stop right now, turn to Appendix I and read the Declaration of Independence.

This extraordinary document relies on legal authority only in the vague reference to Natural Law, but it screams moral authority. Men, inherently, are free! Men can pursue happiness and establish governments which ensure their safety. Men can alter or abolish governments (but should do so prudently and after long sufferance, not for "transient causes"). This is revolutionary rhetoric, the kind for which unsuccessful zealots are hanged.

In fact, just after it warns that men should restrain themselves from hasty action, the Declaration proclaims, in the most hyperbolic fashion, the wrongs the colonies have endured as a petition for sympathy from "a candid world." While the Enlightenment champions reason, the Declaration is also a passionate document. Its imagery is organic, pulsing with energy as it describes the transgressions of the Tyrant King: He has caused legislative bodies to meet in uncomfortable and distant places "for the sole purpose of fatiguing them into compliance"; he has "plundered our seas, ravaged our Coasts ... [and has hired] foreign Mercenaries to compleat the works of death, desolation and tyranny ... ; He has constrained our fellow citizens ... to become the executioners of their friends. ..." It even appeals to fear and racial prejudice: The King has exposed the colonies' frontiers to "the merciless Indian Savages, whose known rule of warfare, is an undistinguished destruction of all ages, sexes and conditions."

This Declaration is alive. The unalienable rights of life, liberty and the pursuit of happiness are secured for men by governments which men themselves establish. The form of government is that which is most likely to produce safety and happiness, and if the government doesn't do that, it is the right and the duty of the people to overthrow it. What an amazing notion! It is a challenge, really. It commands you to own your government, to control your life and the methods by which you live it. It contemplates no excuses, serves up no hiding place. By the way, this is not a blindly laudatory cheer leading session for a document that equates Indians with savages. It is an opportunity to decide what it says about *your life* today.

Laws pronounce what men have said is legal. The Declaration of Independence tells us what is right. It is more than law; it is the self-evident description of the moral imperative. Men are free, and government can't interfere with that freedom. It's a remarkable document, and one which we seldom read, let alone analyze.

We will return to the Declaration of Independence later, but consider these questions as we proceed: What is "the protection of divine Providence" that the Declaration invokes in its concluding sentence? To what extent does this radical rant justify civil disobedience or even revolution within our country today? What ethical notions for living together in a community are compelled by this document?

3

Can a philosophy which is rooted so firmly in Western culture accommodate our increasing sensitivity to our multiple cultural roots?

The Constitution

For four months, from May 25, 1787, to September 17, 1787, thirty-nine delegates from twelve states shaped a new union among the colonies. They quickly scrapped the Articles of Confederation which had loosely and inadequately bound them since 1781. They adopted, instead, a Constitution composed of seven articles, the first three of which establish the branches of government: legislative, executive and judicial. This separation of powers, a system of checks and balances, was a radical departure from previous forms of government.

Instead of a top-down structure in which the king controlled all functions of government, this was a bottom-up system in which the people, through separate and competing departments, would rule. It was consistent with the principles of God-given individual rights articulated in the Declaration of Independence. It stemmed in part from the Enlightenment faith in reason and in part from the suspicion with which the colonies had viewed the British Crown. They recognized under the loose and ineffective Articles of Confederation that national sovereignty was necessary to control trade between the colonies, to establish an effective army and navy and to tax, build postal roads and enforce laws. Thus, Congress was given the power to lay and collect taxes, pay debts, and provide for the common defense and the general welfare *as long as* those taxes were uniform among the states. (They distrusted each other in almost equal measure as they distrusted the Crown.) Article Two made the president commander-in-chief of the army and navy *and* of all the militia of the several states when they were called into service of the United States. The president could appoint judicial officers, ambassadors and public officials. It was up to the president to see that the laws were faithfully executed.

The judicial power, as established in Article Three, was vested in one Supreme Court and such inferior courts as Congress creates. The most important protections of the integrity and independence of the judiciary were life appointments ("during good behavior") and a prohibition against reduction of salary during the time a judge was in office (an abuse of which the Declaration of Independence complained). The crucial judicial power we recognize today, that of declaring legislation or executive action void as contrary to the Constitution, is not specifically stated. It first appears in Chief Justice John Marshall's opinion, *Marbury v. Madison*, (5 U.S. 137 [1803]). Constitutional law to this day continues to define the scope of judicial review of the executive and legislative branches, but *Marbury* was the first case to affirm that when Article Six of the Constitution declares it the supreme law of the land, that means the Supreme Court can and will judge all governmental actions against that standard.

Article Four deals with relations between the states and guarantees that each of them shall have a republican form of government, i.e., one where power is with the people through their elected representatives. Article Five contemplates amendments to the Constitution, Article Six establishes the Constitution's supremacy over other laws and Article Seven provides for ratification.

The First Amendment to the U. S. Constitution [plate 1] says:

> Congress shall make no law respecting an establishment of religion, or prohibiting the free exercise thereof; or abridging the freedom of speech, or of the press; or the right of the people peaceably to assemble, and to petition the Government for a redress of grievances.

Memorize it. Recite it to yourself; turn it over in your mind. Make it a part of your being. We memorize almost nothing in this electronic age. Our loss. Memorization establishes priorities. It says, "Because I am taking the time to inscribe this knowledge indelibly in my mind, it is important to me." Memorization requires discipline and, if we memorize profound passages, instills principles by which we can live and make decisions. Memorization teaches and utilizes the mind's peculiar ability to learn when we are not looking, to make connections when we least expect them and to train our ear to hear the surprise and melody of our language. It preserves the oral tradition and enhances all other learning, because memory builds the shelves on which we store fragments of experience, unformed thoughts and feelings we don't know what to do with. Your head is the most fantastic computer yet invented, and it is, you hope, permanently attached, always with you and capable of making connections which are the stuff of genius. Memorize the First Amendment and ponder the meaning of the five freedoms it protects.

All of the other amendments are important, but the only other one immediate to our inquiry is the Fourteenth, which says in part:

> ... No state shall make or enforce any law which shall abridge the privileges or immunities of citizens of the United States; nor shall any State deprive any person of life, liberty, or property, without due process of law; nor deny to any person within its jurisdiction the equal protection of the laws.

This amendment extends the protection of the First Amendment (and the rest of the first ten amendments which we call the Bill of Rights) to everything the states and local jurisdictions, such as cities and counties, do.

We are a nation of laws, not men. No one, from the president to the most unremarkable citizen, is above the law. Three of our founders—John Jay, Alexander Hamilton and James Madison—in arguing for adoption of the Constitution explained the necessity of a strong government and the perils of a weak one. These essays, called *The Federalist Papers*, praise man's capacity for justice when empowered by a free government, at the same time that they recognize that man's opposite capacity for greed, cowardice and cruelty makes strong government necessary.

Our politics, therefore, is governed by law, just as football is played by rules. In politics, we are the referees, deciding just how much illegal use of the hands we will allow before throwing the yellow flag (no reference to any current politician intended).

For completeness, then, here are the other sources of law in our country. Each state has a constitution, and typically in state matters, one must look to that constitution before seeking relief under the U.S. Constitution. In some cases, the protections afforded to the individual are greater under the state constitution than under the federal constitution. For example, in 1987 the Oregon Supreme Court held that obscene expression is protected speech under the Oregon constitution, which disallows any law "restraining the free expression of opinion", or "restricting the right to speak, write, or print freely." (See *State v. Henry* 732 P. 2d 9 [Or. 1987].) Under the U.S. Constitution, the three major exceptions to First Amendment protection are unlawful speech, such as bribery, forgery, perjury and fraud; speech leading to a clear and present danger; and obscenity under the *Miller v. California* (413 U.S. 15 [1973]) test.

Just remember, in case of a conflict between laws, the U.S. Constitution, as the supreme law of the land, controls.

After federal and state constitutional provisions, we look to federal and state laws as made by Congress and the fifty state legislatures, and federal and state court-made law found in the published decisions of those courts (which guide the decisions of other courts in those jurisdictions). We then look to federal and state administrative rules (such as those of the U.S. Department of Labor) which, when made in accordance with standardized procedures, have the force of law. We also look to local jurisdictions, such as regional governments, counties, cities and parishes, all of which make laws. We are also subject to the demands of sewerage districts, water districts, school boards and a beehive of administrative regulations from federal and state entities dealing with our environment, our buildings, our automobiles and the fabric in our underwear.

Governing the Lawmakers

With this welter of laws, no wonder we are tempted to feel oppressed, frustrated and disgusted with our government. Still, we do own it and if it needs fixing, we can do it. What's required here is responsibility for knowing the issues, voting, and involving one's self

7

in politics—if not as a candidate, then as a knowledgeable advocate on important issues. The framers of the Constitution and Declaration of Independence knew that involvement, challenge and accomplishment, not unearned leisure or disengaged selfishness, lead to happiness. In classical Athens, each citizen was expected to take his turn in government office. A few states still have "citizen legislatures," and even though most politics is now a profession, it will be a noble one only if we truly perceive politicians as working for us. Not to have an *informed* opinion on the critical issues that face us, from the treatment of criminal offenders to the education of all children, is to abdicate our responsibility. It may be helpful to visualize our government as a square, with the Constitution and Declaration of Independence forming the foundation (see Figure 1). Freedom is the goal on the left side (the legal side), and responsibility is the desired result on the right side (the moral or ethical side).

Rights such as free speech, jury trial and security from unlawful searches can be enforced. Responsibilities such as fairness, hospitality toward our fellow citizens, and involvement in our

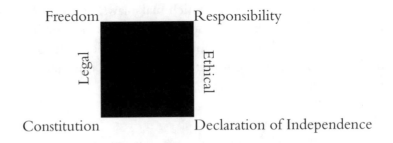

FIGURE 1

government cannot arise not from the injunctions of the law, but from a fundamental understanding of government. Thomas Paine, the great pamphleteer of the revolution, articulated the golden rule of democracy: "He that would make his own liberty must guard even his enemy from oppression; for if he violates this duty, he establishes a precedent that will reach himself." We imperil our own quest for a good life, for liberty and for happiness if we don't protect each other.

The Declaration of Independence and the Constitution, law and morality, freedom and responsibility—each is unfulfilled without its mate. When we don't have time to read the newspaper, we set ourselves up to be victims of our ignorance, our lethargy and our distraction. When we choose not to educate ourselves so that we can articulate arguments rather than just opinions on significant issues, we resign ourselves to things as they are, to the inertia of government by historical accident and to politics as a spectator sport. The fundamental characteristic of an independent citizen is that of an independent thinker, but such thinking is seldom easy and often messy. As the great track coach Bill Bowerman said: "You can't do the long jump without getting sand in your shorts."

There's a little drill you can do to test both your knowledge and your tolerance. If you like Rush Limbaugh, listen to Howard Stern for a day and see if you can articulate his arguments. If Pat Robertson makes you want to retch, watch him anyway and then paraphrase his position. Same with Bill Moyers and Bob Dole and Bill Clinton. Not only will you be sharpening your focus on important issues, you also will be avoiding the increasingly prevalent trend toward listening or watching or reading only those with whom we think we agree. Monolithic thinking, in a democracy, is a recipe for disaster.

The Threat of Order

How can order be a threat to democracy? Wasn't domestic tranquility one of the reasons the Constitution was adopted in the first place? Of course. Anarchy is the absence of order, and governments are established to maintain enough order that people are safe, laws are enforced and freedom is protected.

American government is filled with tensions, however, and this is another: the balance between order and freedom. The concept of the Constitution, and particularly of the First Amendment, is that the goals of equality, life, liberty and the pursuit of happiness are best achieved with minimal interference from the government. As our lives become increasingly complicated, we have used government to address inequities by instituting welfare systems, taxation, health regulations and dozens of other intrusions on both a free-market economy and our individual liberty. Whether these intrusions are good or bad, necessary or not, is not our immediate query, but rather the question: How far can we invite our government into our lives before we alter the balance between freedom and order?

Our square of the Constitution and Declaration of Independence is on a fulcrum, with order on the other end. To the extent we demand more order, we necessarily decrease both our own responsibility for running our government and our individual liberty. It looks like this:

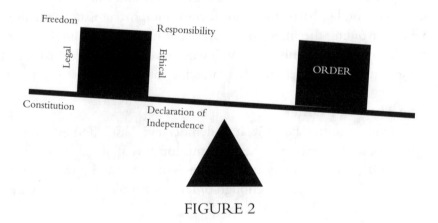

FIGURE 2

The great threat in the republics of the former Soviet Union, now that they have thrown off the tyranny of communism, is that freedom will be too slow, too disorganized, too frustrating, and the people will choose, instead, to sacrifice their freedom to restore order. The key in America, as well as there, is to achieve the proper balance, and that balance may differ from time to time, depending on our needs and problems. Citizen involvement is essential. If we check out and simply don't pay attention to our responsibilities under freedom, we have already voted for order. We have, in effect, said: "I will let someone else be responsible for my life."

Emphasizing ownership to instill a sense of obligation to country makes more sense than implanting a sense of responsibility through guilt or fiat. We keep up our possessions—for example, our clothes or our cars—because we want to preserve their value and usefulness. We serve our country for the same reason. Some form of universal public service, either military or civilian, would enhance rather than diminish our sense of owning our democracy. John Kennedy reminded us that the proper question is not what our country can do for us, but what we can do for our country.

Democracy is improvisation. It proceeds on the assumption that no one knows enough to make irrevocable decisions, so that everything is in a continual state of flux. It puts aside the desire to be secure in favor of the privilege to be free. As political commentator Lewis Lapham observes:

> [Democracy] gives its citizens the chance not only of
> discovering their multiple glories and triumphs but also
> of surviving their multiple follies and crimes. Too of-
> ten we forget the proofs of our courage. If we wish to
> live in a state of freedom, ... then anxiety is the cost of
> doing business.

Anxiety, the fear of the unknown, is, in the words of the writer Walker Percy, "a summons to authentic existence." It is a pebble on the road we follow in pursuit of happiness.

Around this country—in Wheeling, West Virginia, and Lowell, Massachusetts, and Montgomery, Alabama, and Boise, Idaho—people say: "This is the best place in the country to live." They have invested in the success of their local community, or of their neighborhood, or even of their block. When it's somebody else's city and somebody else's government and somebody else's country, then we have become subjects, not citizens. What we learn is that the pursuit of happiness is a collective as well as an individual goal.

Leaders

Now that we have memorized the First Amendment and we have in mind the moral and legal supports of the democratic square as illustrated in Figure 1, how do we choose a politician to lead us? Consider these characteristics of the leader which, I submit, should also be characteristics of us as citizens:

1. Leadership is self-nomination. No one knows better than you about your unique blend of interests, talents and training. Why wait for the accident of discovery?
2. Leadership is intuition. The information explosion often means we have less usable knowledge rather than more. Electronically we can find everything that has ever been written about a given subject, but as critical as that knowledge is, it seldom tells us what to do. A leader's mix of reason, intuition and timing or her ability to understand that which cannot be articulated exactly sets apart the great leader from the common one.
3. Leadership is leading from the rear as well as from the front. The most successful leadership often pushes officeholders toward what they should be doing. That's why the characteristics of a political leader are also the characteristics of a citizen.
4. Leadership is steadfastness—the willingness to hang in there when times are tough because, in some way, they always are.

5. Leadership is humor, which in turn is the saving grace of our civilization.
6. Leadership is flexibility. Situations change, the unexpected happens, and we must deal with it.
7. Leadership is compassion. If a leader is unable to put herself in the position of another, to understand fellow human needs and fears, then how can she promote the common good?
8. Leadership is the ability to motivate others, to talk in word pictures, to bring people along toward a common vision, particularly when that vision requires sacrifice or investment for long-term gain.
9. Leadership is a sense of what is real and a vision of what can be accomplished. Henry Ford said, "Those who believe they can do something and those who believe they can't are both right."
10. Leadership is mistakes. No one in a position of leadership has avoided mistakes. No less a genius than Albert Einstein warned that "a person who never made a mistake never tried anything new." But just as we can never have true freedom without the freedom to fail, so learning from mistakes is another characteristic of a leader.
11. Leadership is trust. Without a fundamental belief in the goodness of people who are empowered, government becomes tyranny, not democracy.
12. Leadership takes no credit and, as a corollary, probably will not get any either.
13. Leadership listens.
14. Leadership takes the heat. As a result, no leader lasts forever. The greatest of leaders, Winston Churchill, got tossed out after World War II by a British populace chafing at the uncomfortable shrinkage of its economic power.
15. And finally, leadership is service and the leader is a servant. The leader serves those who chose her and serves the principles of freedom and equality that the Declaration of Independence and the Constitution describe.

No one commands all of these traits all of the time, nor are they the only ones that describe a leader. But we all possess them to sufficient degree that we can be leaders in our school, neighborhood, city, county and nation.

Who owns the government? We do.

The Rules of Politics

If we own the government (and, remember, the Preamble of the Constitution begins "We the people ..."), then what rules are we going to set up to guide those people who work for us: the politicians? The common wisdom in Washington, D.C., is that for the first six years a congressman represents his district to Washington and thereafter represents Washington to his district. Indeed, the most common way for an incumbent to lose is to get out front on a controversial issue. If one wants to stay in congress forever, do nothing, take no stands, find the parade and get out in front of it; be a demagogue, not a leader.

In a recent discussion of presidential elections by journalists and political consultants, one panelist argued that "anything is fair game if it can be corroborated," another said that the record of anyone who would be president is under a microscope from age five on, and a third said that "character" may be the most important political issue of all. Do we, the people, agree? Is there no standard of relevancy? Must every accusation be answered, every titillation satisfied, every rumor dignified? If character is an issue, what about lying? What about our demanding only reasonable promises and then remembering whether they have been honored? What about fundamental fairness in treatment of the opponent's record, statements and platform? What allegiance should we give to a candidate who is unwilling to address serious public issues? Can we recognize others by the worth of their ideas as opposed to their party labels? The famous judge Learned Hand wrote:

> ...That community is already in the process of dissolution where each man begins to eye his neighbor as a

possible enemy, where nonconformity with the accepted creed, political as well as religious, is a mark of disaffection; where denunciation, without specification or backing, takes the place of evidence; where orthodoxy chokes freedom of dissent; where faith in the eventual supremacy of reason has become so timid that we dare not enter our convictions in the open lists, to win or lose.[1]

We can set rules. We can make known our expectations. The presidential debate in 1992 in which Bush, Clinton and Perot answered questions from an audience of citizens is a start. Requiring presidential candidates to endorse and run on party platforms would be a start. As it is now, platforms represent nothing but an exercise in futility, signifying nothing, standing for nothing, heeded by no one. Perhaps a state could say, "Our primary is on issues only, no presidential candidate's name will appear on the ballot. Come and try to persuade us how we should vote on the issues."

We should pay attention to public character as opposed to private morality. Martin Luther King, Jr. was a man of exemplary courage, exquisite vision and consummate fairness in public life. What he did in private doesn't alter his public achievement. Conversely, Richard Nixon seemed to be a good family man, but he breached his public trust. That matters a lot. Because the process is slow and cumbersome, it is all the more important that we elect leaders who can clearly articulate a vision so that we have something to hold on to as a polestar while the process is adjusting itself.

Our leaders ought to encourage us to assemble and talk to each other about our differences and our commonalties and how we can live with the greatest tension of all in our democracy—the tension between protecting individuality and maintaining commonality. Leaders who live within the truth—that is, who conscientiously gather facts, and know when to act and speak, and then do so on the basis of what they know and intuit, and nothing more—can be the norm, rather than the exception, if we demand it.

Make your own list. And change it as you change and your world changes. Perhaps a government has no soul, conscience or memory, but you do. We can heed the ancient wisdom of Confucius:

> ... wanting good government in their own states, they first established order in their own families; wanting order in the home, they first disciplined themselves; desiring self-discipline, they rectified their own hearts; and wanting to rectify their hearts, they sought precise verbal definitions of their inarticulate thoughts (the tone given off by the heart) ... [2]

Questions for Discussion

1. *The Declaration of Independence states that all men are created equal. Discuss equality in terms of the realities of day-to-day living as you observe life. To begin, think about as many relationships as you can: child-adult, student-teacher, employee-employer, friend-friend, sibling-sibling, male-female, rich-poor and so forth. How might a person's sense of equality change as a relationship changes? For example, during 15 hours, one might in turn be an employee, sibling, spouse, parent, child and student. How does equality factor in during these changing roles?*

2. *The Declaration of Independence states that you have certain un-alienable rights: life, liberty and the pursuit of happiness. What responsibilities accompany having such rights? Discuss these responsibilities in relationship to private settings (home, office) and public settings (buildings, roadways, worksites). Then consider individual rights versus group rights.*

3. *The Declaration of Independence concludes with "reliance on protection of divine Providence." What is this protection? Do people today rely on this protection? Cite evidence to support your position. Is such a phrase consistent with the First Amendment prohibition of state-established religion?*

4. *Is the Declaration of Independence merely an outdated vestige of male-dominated, exclusionary culture?*

5. *What social or political issues, if any, would justify rebellion today?*

6. *Discuss top-down versus bottom-up government in terms of efficiency and equality. Find examples of both styles in your day-to-day life.*

7. *Examine Figure 1. How does this figure change if special interest groups control the making of laws? Read* Federalist No. 10 *and discuss Madison's concerns about the structure of government.*

17

8. *Examine Figure 2. Is this figure an accurate representation? Would you change it? If so, how?*

9. *Are issues such as health care, NAFTA and the federal budget too complicated for citizens?*

10. *How can we restore responsibility and encourage participation in politics?*

11. *Name some leaders you admire. What characteristics set them apart?*

12. *What risks does someone take when running for office? Should every issue be fair game? Should personal lives be examined?*

13. *Can an ethical person be in politics? Can a Christian or Jew or Buddhist hold office and serve the faith? Should a neo-Nazi be allowed to run for office. Discuss these and other related issues.*

Sources

The Constitution, The Bill of Rights, and the 14th Amendment

The Declaration of Independence

Frohnmayer, John. *Leaving Town Alive*. New York: Houghton Mifflin, 1993.

Glendon, Mary Ann. *Rights Talk*. New York: The Free Press, 1991.

Hamilton, Alexander, and James Madison and John Jay. *The Federalist Papers*, ed. Clinton Rossiter. New York: Mentor Books, 1961.

Lapham, Louis H. *The Wish for Kings: Democracy at Bay*. New York: Grove Press, 1993.

Matthews, Christopher. *Hardball*. New York: Harper Perennial, 1988.

---

[1] Judge Learned Hand, Speech, Convocation of the Board of Regents, University of the State of New York, Oct. 24, 1952.

[2] Confucius, *The Great Digest*, trans. Ezra Pound (n.p.), 1947.

Chapter Two

ETHICS

ON OCTOBER 3, 1993, in Mogadishu, Somalia, 18 Americans were killed and 75 wounded after their mission, which was to capture 24 of General Aidid's followers, had nearly succeeded. American troops were in Somalia as a part of a United Nations peacekeeping force prompted by widespread starvation and civil disorder. At this point, General Aidid, a rebel leader, was in hiding, and American strategy was to capture his lieutenants so that he would be forced to take a more visible role. After intelligence identified when Aidid's followers were meeting, a mission was mounted by Army Rangers under American command. They coordinated their activities with the United Nations leaders. Since a helicopter could not land among the closely built structures, the Rangers slid down ropes and accomplished their mission of taking the captives and putting them in vehicles. They were ready to depart when the lead helicopter was shot down by a rocket-propelled grenade.

Then, in what *The New York Times* called "a display of valor," a group of about 100 soldiers formed a perimeter around the downed helicopter to protect the body of the dead pilot, which was pinned in the wreckage. The lightly armed rangers began to take heavy fire from rocket-propelled grenades and AK-47 rifles. They easily could have fought their way out after the convoy left with the prisoners, but they were determined not to abandon the body of the pilot, which they could not free without cutting tools. During the next 12 hours, numerous Americans were killed and wounded. Almost as an afterthought, the article reported that 300 Somalis, including civilians, were killed and 700 wounded in the fierce firefight. The Rangers' creed required each soldier "to complete the mission though I be the lone survivor, and never to leave a fallen comrade to fall into the hands of the enemy."

"War," one officer said, "is not a matter of cost accounting."

How do we deal with this example? Is there some ratio of American lives that equates to other peoples' lives? In war or its equivalent, what happens to ordinary moral standards? Do we, in what is supposed to be a peacekeeping mission, have a right to protect a dead American at the cost of 300 Somalis who are now dead? Do we, as individual citizens and leaders, have the ethical tools with which to evaluate this incident? Was Thomas Jefferson right when he said that there is but one code of morality for men, whether acting singly or collectively?

Here's another example. We look to the law, both on a local and national basis, to give us some guidance on how to act, but often it lends precious little aid. Consider the Pennsylvania Supreme Court case of *Yania v. Bigan* (155 A. 2d 343 [Pa. 1959]), in which Yania was invited onto Bigan's strip-mining property to discuss business. Bigan asked for help in starting a water pump that was in a deep cut filled with 8 to 10 feet of water. At the urging or taunting of Bigan, Yania jumped into the water from a height of 16 to 18 feet and drowned. His estate sued, charging that Bigan was negligent in taunting Yania to jump, failing to warn him of a dangerous condition (the deep water) and failing to go to his rescue. Should Bigan have aided Yania? Is he responsible for his failure to do so? Not at all, responded the court. Bigan didn't physically push Yania, and merely tricking an adult into jumping states no claim. Moreover, that the water could be dangerous was obvious, and the mere fact that Bigan observed Yania in a position of danger imposed no legal responsibility to rescue him.

Outrageous, you say, and indeed it is from a moral standpoint. But the result is consistent with the laws of most states, which do not require one to be a Good Samaritan or to aid another, except when a particular relationship creates a legal duty. In U.S. jurisprudence, we have created a gulf between law and morality which prevents us from looking at the whole human being, the whole society, and indeed our obligations to the whole planet and its inhabitants. Moreover, we are not a society which is consciously struggling with ethical problems. This is not because we lack problems, but because our ethical vocabulary is worn out, our precepts are tattered and our common ethical beliefs are badly in need of rearticulation. We are unwilling or unable to analyze, but—more fundamentally—we are unable even to gather adequate facts upon which to make sound moral decisions. Instead, we moralize in sound bites. We will, I suspect, shortly see an American movie depicting the incident in Mogadishu portraying the American Rangers as heroes (two have received the Congressional Medal of Honor posthumously). The other lives lost (particularly those of the Somali civilians we were there to help) don't seem to register with us. Unquestionably the American soldiers were brave, but did their bravery serve a worthwhile goal? Could the loss of life have been prevented if both ethical and political goals were clear before the battle, the mission, the war, started?

What Is Ethics?

Ethics is the struggle of humans, from the dawn of civilization to the present, to evaluate their actions. It involves putting the immediate situation into a universal context. It is a process that aids in decision-making and in identifying the community to whom the decision is addressed. Ethics evaluates free choices and aids us in living honorably and well. It deals with interhuman relations, because, as the German phrase puts it, "Ein Mensch ist kein Mensch"—a solitary man is no man at all. Ethics preserves the right to choose by requiring responsible action. It studies right and wrong, good and evil, virtue and vice.

A fundamental question in ethics is where to start. One place is religion. In Western theology, many religious systems are positivist.

That is, they start by declaring an axiom such as "God is love." Thus, the greatest good is love, and sin consists in defying God by not loving. What flows from this are the rules (commandments, if you will) or—for some theologians—the rejection of rules. For example, St. Augustine said: "Dilige et quod dis, fac"—Love with care, and then do what you will. Notice that he did not use "amor" or "caritas," but rather chose the Latin word that we would translate as "diligence."

Some ethical systems spring from observation of the natural world. The Hopi Indians, for example, live with a dynamic order that includes the individual, the complex cooperative society that mirrors natural order and the elaborate symbolism that describes it. The individual's duty is to further the Hopi way. Natural phenomena are often given spiritual qualities, as are certain animals. The notion of stewardship of the earth is one which, in today's world, sounds a particularly responsive chord.

A third ethical model might be what we would call classical, remembering the injunction: "First of all, do no harm." Here the ethicist would construct a sliding scale of urgency to determine when action is required. That scale would look at the possibility of harm to others, how likely that harm was, how extensive it might be, the long-term consequences (to the individual and society), how difficult it would be to give aid, who else might be able to and the cost to self or others. Such a system might result in an elaborate set of rules and equations for evaluation of action and could lead to a paralyzing rigidity of the type Mark Twain observed when he said: "He was a good man in the worst sense of the word."

A fourth model is the utilitarian one (i.e., the greatest good for the greatest number), or—differently stated—the maximizing of pleasure and minimizing of pain. Here the philosophers David Hume, Jeremy Bentham and John Stuart Mill might use economic analysis to aid decision-making.

Some philosophers simply declare ethics a waste of time. The French existential philosopher Jean-Paul Sartre acknowledged no generally valid ethical principles, and Sigmund Freud saw ethics as the result of our own super-ego, our conscience which, in childhood, is formed by the Oedipal desire.

What a mess. We seem, as a society, to be ethically paralyzed. While forty-some percent of our citizens might attend church on a regular basis in some communities, the ethics taught there are not readily apparent in our secular, political and economic life. And many individuals have discarded the ethical dimension entirely. In a recent meeting, a business executive turned to a Baptist minister and remarked, "You use ethics in your job all the time, but I seldom do." An astounding statement, but it may be true for most of us. Nature abhors a vacuum, and in the place of firm ethical guidance in our social and political endeavors, we have instead such noxious weeds as college speech codes, legislation to curb violence on television, constitutional amendments to allow prayer in the schools, content restrictions on the work of artists, statutes prohibiting the burning of flags and an unending list of grievances, none of which will be solved by legislation. Moreover, our treatment of each other has become increasingly rude, from hate-filled public exchanges to athletes maiming each other to young people shooting it out on our streets.

America's First Principles

If we in the United States want to be ethically authentic in our public life, we must look to our first principles for guidance. The Declaration of Independence states two propositions from which ethical action can begin. The first is that a people—a nation—can assume a separate and equal status among other nations of the world. The second is that all men are created equal and that they are endowed by their Creator with certain unalienable rights, including life, liberty and the pursuit of happiness. These are bold assertions, but it is unlikely that even our founders believed them absolutely. How could the thirteen colonies, new of origin, weak in numbers, feeble economically, and with a makeshift militia and no navy even pretend to equality with the great European nations of England, France and Spain? And if men are indeed created equal, and their rights, which cannot be taken away, include liberty, then how can one man hold another in slavery? If we are to champion the Declaration of Independence as a fundamental ethical document for today, don't we have some explaining to do about this nation's honesty to itself?

24

The answer is, of course, yes. The great paradox of America is the difference between our ideals and our ability to carry them out. Life, liberty and the pursuit of happiness did not extend to the American Indian, the Negro—either before or after slavery—or the Asian. Women couldn't even vote until ratification of the Nineteenth Amendment in 1920. After World War II, when the United States had become more than equal to the nations of the rest of the world, our respect for the equality of less powerful nations seldom prevented our self-justified invasions. Think, for example, of Grenada, Panama or Cambodia.

Does this mean the Declaration of Independence, tarnished by such transgressions, cannot give us inspiration? It depends on whether we believe what it says. The absolute principles of life and liberty and our own pursuit of a happy life have been abridged and ignored, but never forgotten. It is our willingness, if we can find it within ourselves, to renew our dedication to those principles that stands as the great starting place to which we can return time and again to renew our national spirit and recalibrate our ethical compass.

One difference between ethics and politics is that ethics, being founded on ideals, sets inherently unreachable goals. Politics, on the other hand, being about the accumulation and use of power, often sets no goals at all.

Nothing about remembering our ethical foundations will be easy. Some youth have already disclaimed this nation as living a lie, as holding nothing for them. Consider the words from "Know Your Rights" by The Clash:

> You have a right not to be killed.
> Murder is a crime.
> Lest it's done by a policeman.
>
> ———
>
> You have the right to food money.
> Provided you don't mind a little investigation, humiliation.
> And if you cross your fingers hospitalization.

———

You have a right to free speech.
As long as you're not dumb enough to actually try it.
Know your rights.

———

Get off the street.[1]

Buying into a proposition of equality of opportunity will be as difficult for them as will be the realization, for those who hold real political and economic power, that they will have to share some of that power if all are to participate. But unless we find a common starting place for reuniting our national spirit, we cannot begin the task of acting ethically. And if we cannot act ethically, we cannot authentically pursue happiness, either individually or collectively.

Elasticity is the real genius behind the Declaration of Independence. The document holds within itself the mechanism for change, because it declares that the purpose of government, as instituted among men who are equal, is to secure these fundamental rights which include (but are not limited to) life, liberty and the pursuit of happiness. When government is not achieving that purpose, it is the right of the people to alter or abolish it and institute new government.

Do we believe that this document which declares these fine principles would be heeded once and never again? Remembering that ethics does not exist in a vacuum, but among men, the Declaration of Independence appeals, both at beginning and end, to the opinion of the rest of mankind. In our arrogance as the most powerful country in the world, we have forgotten that we must judge ourselves and be judged by the rest of the world in our allegiance to our own first principles. We needn't beat up on ourselves unduly, but the notion of self-purification, as Martin Luther King, Jr. articulates it in the "Letter from Birmingham Jail," would be a good place to start. This purification has two parts: An admission that our efforts in the past have been less than perfect, and a re-dedication to the principles of equality, life, liberty and the pursuit of happiness for *all* people.

While the purpose of the Constitution is to establish a legal framework for our country, it holds within it certain ethical assumptions. The Preamble shows that establishing justice and the blessings of liberty were fundamental goals. The use of the word "justice" rather than "law" or "order" is a significant statement that what the authors were after was more than a system of laws. They sought to protect a way of life. While it is not the only guide for ethical action in the Constitution, the First Amendment is the wellspring of individual and collective liberty and the continuing source for modification of government that the Declaration of Independence makes mandatory. Thus Congress is forbidden from making any law that would prevent the people from approaching the government and complaining about what they think is wrong. That simple phrase—"to petition the government for a redress of grievances"—contains both the means for change in government policy and the means for peaceful preservation of the government itself.

That the First Amendment can be a basis for ethical action is part of the paradox of the American form of government. The amendment preserves the right to individual conscience. The state will neither declare religion nor prohibit it; only the individual may decide. Speech, press and assembly are prerogatives of free people. The truth that we must relearn on a continuing basis (and this is, indeed, an ethical precept) is that, to the extent we protect other people's religion, speech, freedom to learn and participate in the political process, we preserve our own. This means protecting everyone, not just those belonging to own race, our own gender, our own sexual orientation or our own economic class. If we don't start our ethical journey with the conviction that everyone gets cut into the action, then we live the lie, because both the Declaration of Independence and the First Amendment contemplate that universality. The paradox of freedom is the same as that which characterizes human love: We receive it if we are willing to give it to others.

Using Ethical Principles

The genius of America's first principles is that they anticipate change, recognizing that society matures and the requirements of one generation will be different from those of the next. The famous

27

concurring opinion of justices Brandeis and Holmes in *Whitney v. California* (274 U.S. 357 [1927]) proves both points: It articulates the necessity of change, and it demonstrates that even these courageous and farsighted judges would not, in 1926, declare unconstitutional a law that would probably not pass muster in the conservative court of today. They were considering whether a California statute imposing criminal penalties for participation in the Communist Party violated the defendant's liberty. Here is part of what of they said:

> Those who won our independence by revolution were not cowards. They did not fear political change. They did not exalt order at the cost of liberty. To courageous, self-reliant men, with confidence in the power of free and fearless reasoning applied through the process of popular government, no danger flowing from speech can be deemed clear and present unless the incidence of the evil apprehended is so imminent that it may befall before there is an opportunity for full discussion ...
>
> The remedy to be applied is more speech, not enforced silence ... It is therefore always to Americans to challenge a law abridging free speech and assembly by showing that there was no emergency justifying it.

Earlier in the same opinion they said that our founders valued liberty both as an end and as a means. "They believed liberty to be the secret of happiness and courage to be the secret of liberty." Liberty as a means and an end. Liberty as a legal and an ethical precept. That simple genius of liberty is, through accident of birth, left in each of our hands.

Those who would distinguish law and morality, claiming that the law cannot teach men how to act fairly, give little credit to the power of liberty. Liberty and its siblings, equality, fairness and justice, are what this country stands for, and liberty coaxes its citizens to acknowledge what is not equal, what is not fair, and what is not just and to root them out both in law and in fact. That is the highest calling of our free speech, and particularly of our free press, and that is why justices Brandeis and Holmes saw "an inert people" as the greatest menace to freedom. Ethical action requires courage, self-reliance and involvement.

How can we today do better? How can we promote the reunion of our society? You have already memorized the First Amendment. Now memorize the beginning of the second paragraph of the Declaration of Independence:

> We hold these truths to be self-evident, that all men are created equal, that they are endowed by their Creator with certain unalienable Rights, that among these are Life, Liberty and the pursuit of Happiness. That to secure these rights, Governments are instituted among Men, deriving their just powers from the consent of the governed ...

Aristotle believed that one becomes a moral person by practicing good moral habits. We can only expect to be moral as a nation if we, individually and collectively, practice good moral habits that reflect equality, freedom and respect for life. These traits are accomplished by small steps, minor kindnesses and incidental acknowledgments of the right of another person or nation to be wrong. Here are some questions we can ask ourselves that might aid our reunion with our fundamental principles. You surely can think of more, which will be one sign that you have engaged in your own journey. The important point is that we keep asking ourselves these questions day after day.

> Is what I did today consistent with what I believe?

> Is a policy I am promoting consistent with life, liberty and equality?

> Are we showing respect to the concept of equality among nations?

29

Is the collective pursuit of happiness served?

Did I fulfill not only my own right to speak, but my duty to listen?

Can I fairly restate the argument of one with whom I disagree?

Have I been diligent in fact-gathering so that my position reflects neither moralizing nor hypocrisy?

If I were receiving rather than ordering what I propose, would I think it fair?

Am I prepared not only to admit mistakes I have made, but to take the steps necessary to undo the damage?

When in a position of power, am I willing to leave something on the table?

Can I make the distinction between an adversarial position and a hostile one?

Do my actions reflect personal discipline, restraint and responsibility?

Are the results of my actions unification or division in my society?

You get the point. The harder we work at our society, the better it will be. The great historian Edward Gibbon said: "The winds and the waves are always on the side of the ablest navigators." The more thoroughly we absorb our fundamental principles of liberty and justice and freedom, the fewer hard choices we will avoid, the firmer will be our foundation, the stronger our fabric and the more sure our future.

Questions for Discussion

1. *The Declaration of Independence states the ethical principles that a people or nation can assume a separate and equal status among other nations of the world and that men are created equal with the unalienable rights of life, liberty and the pursuit of happiness. Discuss the Somalia incident in light of these two principles. Consider the incident from the points of view of the American soldiers, the children of those Americans who died defending the already dead soldier, the Somalian soldiers, the children of those Somalian soldiers who died and the Somalian civilians who died. What is the best time to consider ethical issues such as these?*

2. *Discuss the above two principles as they relate to the case of* Yania v. Bigan. *What ethical responsibilities, if any, does an individual have in such a case? Cite examples of similar cases from newspapers, magazines or personal knowledge.*

3. *What system of ethics is at work in your classroom, school, home or community. (See pages 22–24 for examples of systems.) Cite examples to support your position.*

4. *Do you agree with the author that we are sometimes unable to gather adequate facts to make sound moral decisions? Cite examples you have observed, plus newspaper and magazine articles, to support your position.*

5. *Are individual ethics different from group ethics? Cite examples.*

6. *The author states that ethics set unreachable goals, and that politics often sets no goals. Cite examples of how political goals and ethics conflict. How can these differing goals be reconciled?*

7. *The author states that the Declaration of Independence is elastic, having a mechanism for change. Is the current political climate elastic?*

8. *What hypothetical or real circumstances would justify overthrow of the government in accordance with the principles of the Declaration of Independence?*

9. *The author states that those who hold power must share. Cite examples in your life where people share their power. What is the result?*

10. *The author discusses the paradox of Freedom: we receive it if we give it to others. Do you agree with the author? Could we make the same statement for power?*

11. *Use the questions on pages 29–30 to analyze how well you, your school and your nation are doing regarding your ethical growth and understanding.*

Sources

Bellah, Robert N. *Habits of the Heart*. New York: Harper and Row, 1985.

Csikzentmihaly, Mihaly. *Flow*. New York: Harper Perennial, 1990.

Gilligan, Carol. *In A Different Voice*. Cambridge, Mass.: Harvard University Press, 1982.

Ishiguro, Kazuo. *The Remains of the Day*. New York: Vintage International, 1988.

McCollough, Thomas E. *The Moral Imagination and Public Life*. Chatham N.J.: Chatham House Publishers, 1991.

Wilson, James Q. *The Moral Sense*. New York: The Free Press, 1993.

---

[1] The Clash, "Know Your Rights," Combat Rock. Epic Records EK 37689.

Chapter Three

CENSORSHIP AND
ITS PROGENY

*Visual art can pounce on you. ... That's the great thing
about visual art ... its pouncing.*

—Ken Grady, Sculptor

ACKNOWLEDGING THE FREEDOM OF CONSCIENCE that the First Amendment requires us to accept is one thing; actually living with it is quite another. When someone is speaking what we consider blasphemy or disrespect for the flag, our first impulse may be to punch him in the nose, our second is to seek a law that will prevent his behavior. The First Amendment requires just the opposite. It requires us to protect the *right* of the person uttering such words, but it does not require us to agree. In fact, the answer to vicious or wrongheaded speech is always more speech, compelling speech, persuasive speech. The greatest abdication of our duty as citizens is to remain silent in the face of hateful, degrading speech.

Ironically, in spite of the First Amendment, America has a robust history of repression, intolerance and censorship. In fact, the inclination to prevent speech is as old as speech itself. Here is an admittedly superficial romp through the history of censorship. (Note that most of it relates to art which, because it is both speech—the conveying of ideas—and symbol, tends to pack more of a wallop than ordinary words.)

Thinking was what got Socrates in trouble in 399 B.C. He was charged, found guilty and condemned to death for his democratic teachings. The official complaints—"corrupting the young" and "neglect of the gods"—were sufficiently vague that they would have been thrown out on due-process grounds in the United States today. Still, being forced to drink hemlock is censorship at its zenith. Its modern-day equivalent is the death sentence imposed on Salman Rushdie by the late Ayatollah Khomeni, after the former wrote *The Satanic Verses*.

Trifling with the incumbent religious powers could also separate heads from bodies. Take, for example, the Renaissance's super-censor, Girolamo Savonarola, a monk and spiritual ruler of Florence after the exile of the Medici in 1494. In his zeal to clean up the morals of his fellow citizens, he celebrated the "bonfire of the vanities" in the public square, burning books by Boccaccio, poems by Ovid and paintings by Botticelli and Ghirlandaio. When he ignored warnings from the Pope, he was excommunicated and in 1498 executed as a false prophet. Then, for the twenty years between 1545 and 1565, the Council of Trent, with painstaking detail, spelled out the amount of flesh that could be shown on a woman's ankle or hands. This proscription killed the Renaissance. But the Council of Trent wasn't just talk. In 1565 it instructed an apprentice of Michaelangelo, Daniel da Volterra, to cover up the private parts of some of the figures Michaelangelo had painted on the wall above the Sistine Chapel altar [plates 2 and 3]. For his compliance, da Volterra earned the derisive nickname "Il Braghettone"—the breeches-maker.

But even in this repressive age, there were aberrations. Art historian Robert Tine describes the artist Veronese's commission to paint "The Last Supper" in the Church of San Giovanni e Paolo in 1573.

The 42-foot-long mural was to grace the refectory so that the monks, while taking their meals in silence, might have something both entertaining and spiritually enlightening to look at.[1] But Veronese was a hot-blooded Italian, and his "Last Supper," rather than being sedate, formulaic and stylized, instead was filled with beggars, servants, soldiers, a parrot, and a dog—prominently in the foreground—eyeing a cat at Christ's feet. Of course, the Apostles were there, too [plate 4].

The Prior of the church asked Veronese to replace the dog with Mary Magdelene. Veronese refused. The matter came before the Inquisition, and Veronese learned that the dog was the least of his problems. The Inquisition, it seems, was concerned about "Germans" (Inquisition lingo for "Protestants"). A transcript reveals this exchange:

> Q: What is the significance of these armed men dressed as Germans, each with a halberd in his hand? ...
> A: We painters take the same license the poets and jesters take, and I have represented the two halberdiers, one drinking and the other eating nearby on the stairs. They are placed there so they might be of service because it seems to me fitting, according to what I have been told, that the master of the house, who was great and rich, should have such servants.

What about the drunkard, the buffoon, the man with a nosebleed, the apostle picking his teeth, they wondered, and then asked:

> Q: Do you not know that in Germany and in other places infected with heresy it is customary with various pictures full of scurrilousness and similar inventions to mock, vituperate and scorn things of the Holy Church in order to teach bad doctrines to foolish and ignorant people?
> A: Yes. That is wrong; but I return to what I have said, that I am obliged to follow what my superiors have done.

Q: What your superiors have done? Have they perhaps done similar things?
A: Michaelangelo in Rome in the Pontifical Chapel
painted our Lord Jesus Christ, his mother, Saint John,
Saint Peter and the Heavenly Hosts. They are all presented in the nude—even the Holy Virgin—and in
different poses with little reverence.

Enough! Veronese was found guilty and ordered to remove the
buffoons, dog, weapons and "other foolishness" within three months.

What happened? Nothing. After 90 days the Germans still ate
and drank, the nosebleed was unchecked and the parrot interested the
cat. But it was no longer "The Last Supper," said Veronese. It was now
"The Feast in the House of Levi," a less sacred scene and one that,
according to Luke 5:29, contained publicans and sinners. The Inquisition, curiously enough, was satisfied and the painting—dog, parrot,
nosebleed and all—remains to this day for you to see in the Accademia
in Venice.[2]

A celebrated episode took place in Mannheim, Germany, in 1853
where the marble statue of Venus de Milo—the statue herself—was
put on trial, convicted and condemned for nudity [plate 5]. The account of that story does not tell whether she was represented by counsel,
read her rights, asked to testify or even if, without arms, she could
have clothed herself had she suddenly been struck with a fit of un-
scheduled modesty.

In the United States, long before North Carolina's Senator Jesse
Helms raised his censorial head, Thomas Bowdler published the "family" Shakespeare in 1818, in which he attempted to expurgate the
racy stuff (although he didn't catch all of it). Then in 1873, Anthony
Comstock, a New York grocer and religious zealot, championed laws
banning obscene literature from the mails. Comstock's career was long
and ardent—a crusade to protect the nation's youth from "obscene,
lewd and indecent photographs commonly, but mistakenly, called art."
He railed against so-called artists, shielding themselves in the cloak of

free expression while producing material that "fans the flames of secret desires."

Comstock found a congress eager for distraction from a deepening depression, credit scandals and charges of bribes to prominent politicians. (Does this sound curiously contemporary?) Overnight, Comstock was a Washington celebrity and within a short time Congress passed laws prohibiting the selling through the mails or advertising of obscene literature and items "for the prevention of conception." President Ulysses S. Grant named Comstock a special postal inspector and, shortly before his death in 1915, President Woodrow Wilson appointed him to the International Purity Congress. Books and art reproductions were confiscated from booksellers and art dealers. Art schools were raided, particularly if they employed nude models. Comstock helped establish the belief that sexual expression is un-American ("a foreign foe," in his words).

Perhaps predictably then, American painter and muralist Thomas Hart Benton caused a fuss in the 1930s with his paintings "Susanna and the Elders" [plate 6] and "Persephone." As one dismayed viewer exclaimed, "The nude is stark naked!"

Censorship, of course, has not been limited to visual art. In the Middle Ages, the tri-tone in music was such an anathema that it was called "Diabolus in Musica"—the "devil in music"—and the composer Thomas Morley said that it was "against nature." (The song "Maria" from *West Side Story* starts with a tri-tone). The Austrian Archbishop Piffle found Richard Strauss' opera *Salome* so abhorrent when it played in 1905 in Vienna that a restraining action prevented it from being seen again until 1918 [plate 7] In the United States, the Metropolitan Opera's board, after allowing its premiere in 1907, acceded to critics and barred further performances on the grounds that "this diseased" work was "detrimental to the opera's interests."

In the 1920s, the great age when jazz matured, there was an anti-jazz movement to censor this new form of American music. A professor "proved" that pregnant women who listened to jazz were likely to have deformed children. Jazz was viewed by its critics as "decadent," the devil's music and composed of "jungle rhythms." Even serious critics had problems with the art form, stating that since jazz is improvised, it is contrary to discipline. In 1921, Zion City, Illinois, banned jazz performances along with smoking and other sinful practices. In Chicago, no trumpet or saxophone playing was allowed after dark.

You might think the following is an attack on rap music:

> A wave of vulgar, filthy and suggestive music has inundated the land ... with its obscene posturing, its lewd gestures. Our children, our young men and women, are continually exposed ... to the monotonous attrition of this vulgarizing music. It is artistically and morally depressing and should be suppressed by press and pulpit.

Surprisingly not. It is from a musical publication in 1899 railing against the evils of ragtime. Similar apocalyptic pronouncements were made about rock and roll, Elvis and the Beatles in the 1950s and 1960s. Today they seem tame, which is precisely why we should check the natural human impulse to suppress that which inflames us. Two very different values are involved here: The first is to argue forcefully against something, the second is to ban it. The first is absolutely consistent with our freedom. The second undermines it.

The Alaska Experiment

From 1989 to 1992 Robert Mapplethorpe, Andres Serrano and performance artists Holly Hughes and Karen Finley were household names. Congress received more mail on federal funding of the arts than it did on the savings-and-loan scandal, even though the former involved pennies and the latter billions. This culture war is still very much with us, because the conflict between tolerance, on the one hand, and respect for sensibilities and deeply held beliefs, on the other, is totally unresolved. In an effort to bring some sense to this struggle, the Visual Arts Center in Anchorage, Alaska, put together a show of approximately sixty works, all of which had been censored somewhere in the United States in the last several decades. Not all of these censorial acts were First Amendment violations, because not all of them involved governmental action. (Remember, for the First Amendment to apply, the government must somehow be involved with the speech, religion, or assembly in question). But in every instance, someone was attempting to prevent others from seeing an artwork.

The common reasons given for an image's removal were either opposition to the ideas expressed or a desire to protect others—children, for example. The artwork depicted nudes, some provocative and some seemingly innocent; defacing or trampling upon the flag; criticism of politicians and policies; oppression of women; issues of sexuality, including homosexuality, condoms and lesbian art; depictions of intolerance, such as Nazi skinheads and the Ku Klux Klan; pregnant women; body mutilation; and unflattering depictions of ethnic groups. Some of the artists were dismayed by the censorship, and others saw it as a daily fact of life.

The Anchorage show drew more than 2,000 visitors in a three-week period, a record for the Visual Arts Center. The accompanying week-long seminar drew many more. Jann Ingram, writing for the *Anchorage Daily News*, remarked that what was shocking to her was not Mapplethorpe's photos or Dread Scott's flag on the floor, but rather how tame much of the work was. How drugstore employees and police managed to read "sexually explicit" into Alice Simms' lyrical "Water Babies," a nude photo of her baby seeming to float with water lilies [plate 8], totally escaped her. On the other hand, Perry Carr, a columnist for the *Anchorage Times*, opined that the exhibit was "dim witted, vacant and amateurish ... and hoisted bad taste to a level rarely seen."

An index of the success of this project, however, was the amount of public involvement it provoked. The catalyst for that involvement was Dread Scott's four-year-old piece entitled "What is the Proper Way to Display a U.S. Flag?" The School of the Art Institute of Chicago found itself in total chaos when this piece first appeared in a student show in 1988. Expletives and threats filled the comment book, President Bush called the work disgraceful, local legislators passed anti-flag-on-the-floor legislation (later declared unconstitutional), veterans protested, bomb threats were received and the school itself was barely able to function. Even the artistic community was split over the issues of artistic integrity, patriotism and whether the piece was any good as art.

What was this image that stirred such passion? It consisted of an American flag spread on the floor and a small, wall-mounted shelf supporting a comment book in which viewers could respond to the question, "What is the proper way to display a U.S. flag?" Above the shelf was a picture of a flag-draped coffin. To write in the comment book, the visitor could choose to stand on the flag.

The flag art quickly became the focus of the show. At the opening reception, a group of veterans paid the five-dollar admission fee and entered the exhibition. Following prescribed flag etiquette, they picked up the flag, folded it, saluted it, and handed it—along with a book on flag etiquette—to Jan Erickson, the project coordinator [plate 9]. She returned the flag to the floor, saying, "This exhibit is not about disrespect to the flag. It's about the right to free expression. The viewer chooses whether to stand on the flag or not."

The following day, a group of veterans again paid the admission fee to enter the exhibition, but this time they quickly folded the flag and handed Jan Erickson a check for $50, along with a letter stating that the flag was being taken into protective custody. Erickson told them that if they removed the flag, she would have to call the police. Upon leaving the Visual Arts Center, the V.F.W. State Commander and one other man were arrested and charged with larceny, a Class A misdemeanor with a maximum $1,000 penalty. Another flag, purchased by a patron, was placed on the floor within 20 minutes. Erickson said they considered putting glass over the flag or perhaps gluing it to the floor. They checked with the artist in New York, who encouraged them to substitute flags when the original was taken.

The veterans commenced a peaceful protest outside the Visual Arts Center, and inside, the Dread Scott piece did what art is uniquely capable of doing: It quickened people's minds and focused their beliefs. These are some comments from the book:

I feel—it's just material. But also—I was hesitant to do it—I wondered before I did, if I would.

I respect what other people believe this flag stands for. It is out of respect for their feelings that I stand on this flag with my shoes off.

I don't want to walk on it—it was good for me to find this out.

How interesting. I thought folks who objected to this piece were over-reacting, but as I write, I'm standing to the side of the flag. Thanks for the insight and opportunity.

Standing here on the flag, I do feel the power to change the 'what is' to the 'what should be' and do feel a tinge of hope.

For some reason I find I can stand on the stripes but couldn't bring myself to stride over the stars.

I felt unearthed, that is, ungrounded. Dizzy. It's helping me realize just how much meaning I have vested personally in this symbol ... I am getting a closer understanding of the relationship between the symbol, the truth and myself.

I didn't think that I would want to participate in this until I saw all of the works that had been censored—so ridiculous. So here I stand. Who knows—if the Supreme Court says that my body is not mine, I may burn one.

Move the flag off the floor. I was busy looking at the wall and accidentally stepped on it.

A little more than a week after her father was arrested for taking the flag, 17-year-old Robin Brogan stood to the side of the flag and wrote in the book:

> I think this is disgusting. Dread Scott is taking advantage of his rights that my father fought for. The First Amendment only goes so far and this definitely crosses the line ...

Then she scooped up the flag, left a $50 deposit that she had been given by a protester outside, and scurried out of the Arts Center. What followed could only be described as surreal. Robert Pfitzenmeier, a former Visual Arts Center staffer who had returned to Alaska to go fishing, was rollerblading outside and saw her as she ran from the center. He started after her, grabbing her shoulders and coat to stop her. While Pfitzenmeier was chasing Brogan, he was "whipped with an American flag" carried by one of the protesters. "The flag ... was all over my face," he said. Then Ron Siebels, a Vietnam veteran with boxing and martial-arts skills, chased down Pfitzenmeier and threw him to the ground. Police arrived, and Pfitzenmeier was detained, perhaps to protect him from the fifty demonstrators. Siebels later said in a letter to the editor that he was merely rescuing a young woman in distress and didn't act because he was a veteran. Susan E. Palmer, assistant director of the center, lamented that the protesters and supporters "can't hear each other. It's very frustrating."

Another flag was donated, and the next day the game of capture-the-flag continued. Protesters twice paid admission to the Visual Arts Center and emerged with neatly folded American flags, the third and fourth taken. The police made no arrests. After that, a Vietnam veteran brought five U.S. flags to the gallery for use in the exhibit.

In more than seventy-five letters to the editor printed in the Anchorage papers, citizens spoke out. "How can we teach values when we stand on the flag?" asked one. "I resent those who are willing to trample on the Constitution in the name of patriotism, and I'm saddened by those veterans who missed the point of why they were fighting," responded another. "As a veteran I swore an oath to defend the Constitution, not symbols. The Constitution guarantees freedom of speech," said a third.

An Air Force veteran wrote:

> ...When I first arrived I had not intended to stand on this flag at all while I wrote. This is because I respect what it stands for and I understand why the veterans do not call it 'just a piece of cloth.' But by their action [taking the flag] they have rendered this flag *meaningless* and it is only a piece of cloth as long as they suppress the freedom of speech and expression which belongs to all of us. I hope I never have to do this again.

Others thought the display polluted the memory of those who had died. A member of the Alaska State Council for the Arts wrote:

> You are truly a pathetic excuse for an artist. These rights and freedoms you take so lightly aren't free. Rather they were secured by brave citizens who were brought home beneath the very symbol you choose to disrespect. *Being legal* should not be confused with having something worth saying. I feel quite sorry for you and hope that, with time, you might even progress to the point of mediocrity.

What would *you* have done? Recite the First Amendment (which you have memorized) and use it to analyze the following citizen responses. The question is not whether you agree or disagree, but where, if at all, speech becomes action and loses its protected status.

1. We Americans are losing our cherished values by blindly following the 'freedom of everything' minority.
2. I am boycotting the Visual Arts Center.
3. I recommend all citizens counter this disrespectful

display by flying their flags on June 14 (Flag Day).

4. Citizens should rise up against the businesses that sponsor this offensive display.

5. When one steps on the flag he steps on us all. It's a sacred symbol. It's a nerve and it hurts. Laws are made to stop one person from hurting another ...

6. I cheer the Vietnam veteran who confronted a flag burner and said 'if you have the right to burn the flag, I have the right to punch you in the nose.'

7. I support the veterans who removed the flag from the exhibit.

Personal opinion, personal boycotts, countering symbolism with symbolism, economic boycotts and even false logic are protected speech. And perhaps expressing support for violence and breach of the peace are protected, too. But nose-bashing is not a protected First Amendment activity, and while the veterans who took the flags were taking it into "protective custody," had they been prosecuted, the First Amendment would not have saved them from a larceny conviction.

Now analyze these letters to the editor, which were, by the way, in the minority.

1. The veterans who stole the flag should be arrested for theft. It is ironic that a show on censorship should itself be censored [by stealing the flag].

2. The flag is just cloth. It is what it stands for [liberty, expression and choice] that is important.

3. Left to run its course censorship becomes an ideological battleground where every faction of our diverse society attempts to control the thoughts of everyone else.

4. I found the Mapplethorpe to be disgusting. But disgust is within the realm of what's conveyed by art.

5. To make art possible is not to condone it.

Anatomy of a Censor

The show accomplished, perhaps beyond the organizers' wildest expectations, what it intended. The vigorous dialogue lasted well after the show closed. Seeing these works together was a stunning revelation of the anatomy of censorship. The work was so diverse that even the most ardent censors would not have agreed upon what should have been banned. Kriste Lower of The American Family Association, a group vigorously opposed to obscenity said "there are 10 pieces in there that I don't consider art." Amazing. Fifty of the censored pieces apparently passed muster with her. Censorship is whimsical. It is triggered as much by what the censor brings to the work as by what the work, itself, is.

The censor, above all, is impatient. All artwork involves ideas, and the life of a half-baked idea is very short indeed. The censor's zeal often prolongs that life rather than shortening it. For example, Robert Mapplethorpe's photos now sell for $60,000—far above what they brought during his lifetime.

The censor favors order over freedom. Freedom is imprecise, inefficient, ambiguous and often annoying. To the censor, order is of a higher magnitude, particularly when the censoring is done in the name of protection of the young, the impressionable or the sensitive. And once a censor starts, there is no logical stopping point. The censor is a literalist, not seeking context or intended meaning and often not even wanting to know the content of that which he would prohibit. "You don't have to be in the sewer to know that it smells," remarked one. The world is black or white, good or evil, with no shades of gray.

Usually the subject of a censored work is unsympathetic. Nazis, perceived blasphemers and flag-burners are hard to stomach for many people. And yet it is precisely minority opinion, unpopular opinion, that the First Amendment most strenuously protects. The reason is that if we don't protect everybody, then nobody is safe. If we can't win a battle by logical argument and persuasive speech, then America is not safe.

The left of the political spectrum is as intolerant as the right and neither, when it comes to censorship, can claim the moral high ground.

In this show, a substantial number of works did not pass muster with what might be deemed the more liberal side of the political landscape. The KKK robe, the Nazi subject matter or what was deemed by the censor to be an inappropriate treatment of women and ethnic minorities are examples. State-enforced intolerance, whatever its justification, is contrary to our belief in freedom.

The battle over whether an artwork will or will not be allowed to speak its own message is often a battle for public opinion. The arguments that it is too indecent, too blasphemous or too wretched for the public to see are notions that we often find buried in ourselves. They trigger our own internal war over standing up for what we think is good, on the one hand, and defending the rights of others to express their opinions about what they think is good, on the other. A crucial distinction is that, in supporting a person's *right* to speak, we can still vigorously disagree with the message.

Finally, censorship is an issue of control, of power over what others will or will not have the opportunity to experience. Most of us would find censorship irresistible if we were the only ones making the decision. But democracy listens to all voices and exists, always, with the tension that different views produce. The process of speech is the process of growth, of understanding and enlightenment, and like a muscle, speech grows stronger with exercise and atrophies with disuse.

Particularly in times of societal stress, such as economic hard times or political uncertainty, the urge to be ethically pure, morally superior and intolerant of "filth" is almost irresistible. Anthony Comstock and Jesse Helms played to that siren, each in his own generation, and both claimed to be patriots. To the extent they succeed, we all fail, for in the words of the historian Henry Steele Commager: " ... [Censorship] creates, in the end, the kind of society that is incapable of exercising real discretion ... incapable of appreciating the difference between independent thought and subservience."

Prophylactic Measures and Rules of Engagement

How can we protect the First Amendment in the inevitable and necessary debates on divisive issues? For the artist—particularly the artist using public funds—or for the journalist or public-school teacher, there is an obligation to provide some context when confrontational or difficult work is presented. This doesn't mean that the work has to be explained, but rather that some background be available, so that the audience or class can share the artist's creative journey or the teacher's intent in presenting challenging materials. Art instructor Carol Becker, in her lecture at the Anchorage symposium, said: "Nobody talks about audiences in art school. We need to provide students with enough information so they are not afraid of questions." Not all artists seek dialogue, and that is fine. But if an artist accepts public money, then that dialogue is part of the bargain. And the teacher who presents difficult subjects for discussion is doing her job, but the First Amendment better enhances reasoned discussion if the class is (or parents are) not immediately shocked into opposition. Debate, in short, is enhanced by preparation.

Another rule of engagement in art-inspired controversy should be that the work not be taken out of context—that is, that it not be deliberately misunderstood. A fundamental rule of fairness, in both art and ethics, is to get the facts right, insofar as the facts are discernible. Sometimes they aren't. As the philosopher Bertrand Russell pointed out in 1950: "The most savage controversies are those about matters as to which there is no good evidence." Issues of faith are a good example. In politics, however, it is an old and disreputable technique: Misstate your opponent's position, and then attack it relentlessly. It is hard to see, in either democracy or art, how misinformation helps us.

Before a controversial art work is to be presented, the presenter should, by a series of discussions or lectures, remind us of the First Amendment and what it means to protect unpopular ideas and how it helps preserve our ever-evolving democracy. We can't presume that the issues the artists dealt with in the Alaska show were simple or simply resolved. The artist often intentionally juxtaposes the sacred and profane, wades into taboo or challenges the established order. This irreverence, this outrageousness, this grabbing and flaunting our anxieties, seldom goes down easy, and often, as is the privilege of free expression, it is so much drivel and foolishness. But even in its reflection of life's absurdities, art moves us forward as a society, and that is precisely what the First Amendment is meant to allow. Supreme Court Justice William O. Douglas said in 1949 that free speech "... may indeed best serve its high purposes when it induces a condition of unrest, creates dissatisfaction with conditions as they are, or even stirs people to anger. ..."

Controversial work, when presented, ought to be accompanied with an opportunity for dialogue. The symposium in Anchorage and the exchange of letters compel us to respect the strongly held views on all sides of the issue. Hearing those views with which one might violently disagree is a privilege, not a burden, of freedom. In this sense, the artist re-presents the society to itself.

But what about the genuine offense? What about the person who has confronted the work, lived within the truth in examining it, and is morally repulsed nonetheless? The answer is that the First Amendment protects all forms of speech, even those which are repulsive, unless they rise to the level of judicially declared obscenity. Moreover, democracy guarantees no insulation from the unpleasant, the difficult or the annoying. In fact, it demands just the opposite—that we not be islands, but rather that we share the action and passion of our time. Democracy requires self-definition, which is an extension of the strongly individualistic and action-oriented history of Western thought expressed by Rabbi Hillel in the twelfth century:

> If I am not for myself, who will be for me?
> If I am not for others, what am I?
> And if not now, when?

The Alaska show, with all its trials and triumphs is summarized in a single letter to the editor:

> After an emotional protest, the veterans gently picked the flag up from the floor, cradled it lovingly, saluted it, respectfully folded it and handed it back to Jan

Erickson, one of those responsible for the exhibit and the seminars on censorship. I was warmed by the dignity of both the veterans and Erickson as she in turn defended freedom of speech and returned the flag to the floor. It took courage and patriotic conviction for the veterans to march into the VAC and likewise for the center's staff to defend their exhibit. The Visual Arts staff educated us on censorship issues and provided the stage for this performance on democracy. Neither side should be silenced.

Postlogue
You may wonder what happened to the Visual Arts Center after the show. Anchorage mayor Tom Fink vowed to veto its municipal appropriation. In July 1992, a month after the show closed, four members of the Alaska State Council for the Arts supported a motion to cut off all funding for the Visual Arts Center, claiming that the censorship exhibition had offended a majority of Alaskans. Although the motion failed six to four, executive director Verne Stanford and his staff were laid off in late September 1992, and the Visual Arts Center closed. Three months later, its equipment was sold at an auction to help pay a longstanding $100,000 debt. None of those arrested were prosecuted. The Anchorage Visual Arts Center is now only a memory. Perhaps this proves the old adage that no good deed goes unpunished.

Questions for Discussion

1. *Are there circumstances in which censorship is justified?*

2. *Do we need to protect the young and impressionable? If so, how?*

3. *How do we respond to the person who is genuinely offended?*

4. *Should public art be acceptable to the majority? What about minority views?*

5. *Can you give an example of when censorship has been or would be considered appropriate and successful?*

6. *Collect a variety of art books of generally accepted artists that include nudes or other potentially controversial art. Share these books with small groups of students. Remind them of how music that was once considered controversial is now considered acceptable. Have them discuss the art in terms of potential censorship. Make the argument for the censor; the artist; the Visual Arts Center.*

7. *Think about the situation at the Visual Arts Center. Should the flag stealers have been prosecuted?*

8. *Does supporting a show mean that the VAC agrees with the artists viewpoints? Is it possible to truly know an artist's viewpoint?*

9. *Was Robin Brogan (the 17-year-old who took the flag) right? Does the First Amendment only go so far?*

10. *Was it appropriate for the Alaska arts council to retaliate by cutting the budget?*

11. *What do you think would happen if the show were mounted in your community?*

12. *Given that the censored art show led to the permanent closure of the Visual Arts Center, was it worth the cost?*

13. *Is all art speech?*

Sources

Frohnmayer, John. *Leaving Town Alive*. New York: Houghton Mifflin, 1993.

Gablik, Suzi. *The Reinchantment of Art*. New York: Thames and Hudson, 1991.

Heins, Marjorie. *Sex, Sin and Blasphemy*. New York: The New York Press, 1993.

Hentoff, Nat. *Free Speech for Me—But Not for Thee*. New York: Harper Perennial, 1992.

---

[1] Robert Tine, "Artist Outwits Inquisition," *The New York Times* (Nov. 12, 1990).

[2] The entire transcript of Veronese's harrowing brush with the Inquisition is in *Veronese: The Supper in the House of Levi* by Giuseppi Delogue (Transbook Co., Inc., New York/Milan).

Chapter Four

RELIGION AND GOVERNMENT

SCHOOL PRAYER IS A POOR WAY to practice religion and a good way to damage democracy. Still, 60 percent of Americans favor the idea and the U.S. Supreme Court's 1962 decision striking down a 22-word nondenominational prayer (*Engel v. Vitale* 370 U.S. 421 [1962]) is the single most unpopular decision in the last 30 years. The nondenominational prayer, written by the New York State Board of Regents, was not mandatory—the local school boards could choose whether or not it was recited in classrooms each day. Moreover, students could remain silent or be excused from the room if they requested. The prayer, in its entirety, was: "Almighty God, we acknowledge our dependence upon thee, and we beg thy blessing upon us, our parents, our teachers, and our country."

The roles of religion and government, and the ways in which they interact, have caused a clash of titanic proportion. On the one hand are the deepest beliefs of a traditionally God-fearing country, and on the other, the most fundamental principle of our democratic union: that the government must stay out of matters of individual conscience.

According to Justice Black who wrote the decision in *Engel*, the establishment clause of the First Amendment ("Congress shall make no law respecting an establishment of religion ..."), stands as an expression by our founders that religion is too personal, too sacred, too holy to permit its "unhallowed perversion" by a civil magistrate. Religion, in short, is no part of the business of government (and governments run schools, directly or through delegation, and pass laws requiring that students attend).

But equally important is the free exercise clause of the First Amendment ("Congress shall make no law ... prohibiting the free exercise [of religion]"). The two clauses are in dynamic tension, because if each is expansively read, they bump into each other. A government which is taking great pains not to establish a religion may step on the toes of one who is attempting to practice religion. School prayer is an example. Those who oppose it point to the anti-establishment clause and those who promote it say that the free exercise of religion extends to voluntary prayers by students in public schools. How do we find the balance?

A Moral Crisis

Some argue that the law is unsettled on whether student-instigated and student-led prayer at public-school graduations or other school functions violates the First Amendment. The pressure to institute such prayer is substantial. Advocates argue that we are in a moral crisis and values, such as those presented by religion, must again be taught in the public schools. The moral crisis, however, is no justification to jettison the fundamental principles upon which our country was founded. If we do not protect the right of individual conscience, will the religious commitment of the majority ride roughshod over minority views? Even if only one student in the whole school does not voluntarily join in the prayer, will we have eroded our democracy?

Students have never been prohibited from praying in school. Indeed, the old adage goes, "As long as there are exams, there will be prayer in school." In a study hall, a reading period, between classes or at hundreds of other times during the day a student can offer up a prayer in silence, or even out loud, if it will not disrupt or coerce other students. The key here is that the student voluntarily makes the choice. It is a personal one in which the school, as a representative of the government, has no part.

Why, then, do we need an organized moment of silence at the beginning of the school day, as some are urging? If it is so that students can publicly profess their faith by praying silently together, then allowing school time for such an activity can be coercive. What message does it send to the student whose head is not bowed? Would the school, without the urging of organized religion, set aside such time?

The intrusion is even greater when one considers the alliance that is being made with the school. Many have argued that religion is trivialized in contemporary American life through its depiction on television, its seeming irrelevance to our social, ethical and political life, or its ridicule in literature. But how much more trivialized would religion be if it were put in the hands of the state. Thomas Jefferson envisioned a "wall of separation" between religion and government and Madison said that religion is "wholly exempt from [the state's] cognizance." If government based on political power is arrogant, think what it would be were it allied with religious power. Even a student-led and student-initiated prayer would still be at the sufferance and under the control of the school.

And finally, because school prayer must be nonsectarian, unspecific and bland to have even to have a chance of surviving constitutional scrutiny, it is, in fact, only a symbol of a prayer, empty of reference to any meaningful religious experience. The ceremonial invocation of god in nonreligious places, such as schools, is a clanging cymbal that mocks that which it would honor. If we were doing a cost-benefit analysis, the value of such a prayer, either as contact with a deity or as promotion of some sort of moral rebirth is puny, indeed, as weighed against our duty to protect the conscience of those who might not welcome prayer in the secular setting.

Historical Precedent

Our founding fathers struggled with the place of religion in government. After the American Revolution, the Virginia Legislature proposed both the establishment of the Episcopal Church as the state's official religion and a tax to support Protestant religious education to counter sin and immorality in young people. James Madison, in opposition to the religious education bill, wrote his *Memorial and Remonstrance Against Religious Assessments* in 1785. See if you find his arguments persuasive today:

Religion can't be imposed by force. It is an unalienable bond between man and the Creator; it precedes any civil authority or duty and cannot be affected by any man-made law.

Any governmental body venturing into religion oversteps its bounds and can become tyrannical.

If Christian principles can be enforced by a government now, a new majority could enforce other beliefs later.

All men are equal and have an equal right to their own persuasion on religion. If this is taken away, it is an offense against God, who granted this equality.

No civil magistrate is competent to be a judge of religious truth.

Religion doesn't need the state. It can and will flourish without the support of human laws.

Religious establishments, historically, have perverted religion. They have led to pride and indolence of the clergy and servility and ignorance of the laity.

Religion is not necessary to civil government. A sound civil government will protect freedom of conscience in its citizens.

An established religion would be contrary to the general policy of America in offering asylum to the oppressed of every religion and nation. Established religion is, itself, a symbol of persecution.

It would, therefore, discourage immigration.

Religion evokes zeal. "Torrents of blood have been spilt" over states imposing religious opinion. Such laws would destroy the moderation, harmony and forbearance of America.

Such a bill would discourage, rather than encourage, people who were unpersuaded in finding religious truth.

Because such a law would be obnoxious to a great number of citizens, it would undermine civil authority.

A step of such magnitude and delicacy (teaching religion through the state) would require the concurrence of a majority of citizens, and no way has been devised to ascertain that will.

The power of a state legislature is not unlimited. It cannot touch the sacred right of free conscience.

Madison's arguments were persuasive to the people of Virginia and to his fellow legislators. He had also won an equally significant point earlier in persuading James Mason, when writing the Virginia Declaration of Rights in 1776, to eliminate the proposed "all men should enjoy the fullest toleration in the exercise of religion" and in its place to substitute "all men are equally entitled to the free exercise of religion." It was more than a trivial distinction. Toleration suggests that the state should, out of its largesse, forbear. As Thomas Paine put it, the right to tolerate suggests the right to persecute. Free exercise, on the other hand, is consistent with a "God-given right" to individual conscience. It favors the individual over the state in matters of belief.

Utmost Regard for Religion

The restriction on the mixing of politics and religion extends far beyond the singular issue of school prayer. Politics deals in compromise, military power, economic policy and relative choices, while religion addresses absolutes, ideal standards, a Supreme Being and, ultimately, the afterlife. The great twentieth century Christian theologian Reinhold Niebuhr described the dilemma succinctly: "Religion is so frequently a source of confusion in political life and so frequently dangerous to democracy, precisely because it introduces absolutes into the realm of relative values."

He warned against the "evil to which individuals and communities may sink when they try to play the role of God in history." We need look no further than Bosnia, Northern Ireland or Iran to identify the excesses that occur when politics mixes with religion.

Men will differ on issues of ultimate truth. History teaches that lesson just as surely as it warns that when religion and government are too closely allied, religion becomes a source of conflict, death and war. Conversely, when religion stands outside the government and criticizes it in light of absolute standards, religion can be a source of peace, love and mediation in the world. Compare, for example, the Protestant church in Germany from 1933–1945, completely co-opted and silenced by a tyrannical government, with the Negro churches in Montgomery, Alabama, during the bus boycott. The latter spoke forcefully about injustice. The former spoke not at all.

None of this means that religion can have no part in government. Leaders and citizens who profess a faith can and do act on the basis of that faith in their public and private duties. That is the essence of the free-exercise clause. But if religious exercise is truly to be protected, it must stand outside man's all-too-human efforts to govern his world. Otherwise, religion becomes just another political exercise.

The Will of the Majority Versus Individual Conscience

On observing America in the 1830s, the French traveller Alexis de Tocqueville remarked on the religious nature of the American people. He was used to seeing religion devalued as the Age of Reason swept through European governments. But even with the proclivity toward religion in America, he also observed that clerics and lay people alike agreed that religion and government ought to be strictly separated. Tocqueville feared the tyranny of the majority. He wondered whether individual conscience could withstand the tremendous pressure of majority opinion. The third-century Christian writer Tertullian said, "It is no part of religion to compel religion." Yet that is exactly what Tocqueville foresaw—that individual conscience could not withstand majority belief.

Former Librarian of Congress Daniel Boorstin described the spirit to be protected:

> The courage to doubt, on which American pluralism, federalism, and religious liberty are founded, is a special brand of courage, a more selfless brand of courage, than the courage of orthodoxy. A brand that has been far rarer and more precious in the history of the West than the courage of the crusaders or the true believer who has so little respect for his fellow man and for his thoughts and feelings that he makes himself the court of last resort on the most difficult matters on which wise men have disagreed for millennia.[1]

The need to protect others in order to protect ourselves is a common element in all First Amendment issues, as is the conviction that we must protect the articulation of ideas of others which we may think entirely wrong. We are free to attempt to persuade by words, by the timeworn religious device of guilt, by revelation or conversion, but never by coercion at the hands of the state. The issue, as Boorstin points out, is ultimately one of respect—which, if we are trying to reinstill morality within our society, is a good place to start.

Learning to Listen

Many of our deepest beliefs are animated by religion, and so, not surprisingly, many of our significant social issues involve religion as well. Abortion is one example; the death penalty and conscientious objection to war are two more. We could enhance our ability to resolve conflict if we perfected the democratic skill of listening.

At Vanderbilt University in the fall of 1993 Sara Weddington, the lawyer who argued and won *Roe v. Wade* before the U.S. Supreme Court (establishing a woman's right to abortion) and Phyllis Schlafly, a long-time abortion opponent, shared the stage. It was advertised as a debate, but it hardly achieved that dignity, with each speaker sending her well-rehearsed barbs past the other like shells from field artillery. The audience was roughly equally divided, applauding, in turn, statements from the combatants. During the question period, Vanderbilt Assistant Chaplain Gay Welch said: "I would like each of you, as clearly and concisely as you can, to state the position of the other and then turn to her and ask her if you got it right." Neither speaker volunteered to go first, and each needed to be prompted, after a woeful description of the other's position, to ask whether that position had been correctly stated. Of course, it hadn't been, because they were warriors and sought to accomplish the impossible: total surrender from the other side.

Can religion be a mediating force that acts from outside of government to promote the cause of human dignity? Can religion promote a spirit in America that aids the quest for liberty and justice and equality? Absolutely. Religion has filled that role at times in our history, opposing slavery before the Civil War and promoting the social gospel in the early twentieth century, for example. Some would argue that that is what is meant when America is described as a religious nation: that we are informed by the spirit of religion which, in turn, supports the spirit of liberty.

Does government neutrality toward religion mean that it cannot be taught in the public schools? The distinction is between preaching and academics. If we, as a citizenry, had a better understanding of world religions, what motivates men and women at the core of their souls, we might do better in understanding them, predicting their behavior and dealing with them politically. It's a tricky line to draw, however, between doing justice to the role of religion in history by teaching it in a nonpartisan manner on the one hand, and not trying to persuade, on the other. Because religion has become such a legal minefield, schools and governments alike have avoided it entirely rather than to take a chance of offending the law. But the current legal principle, at least as far as the establishment clause is concerned, is that government need not be hostile, merely neutral so that it neither promotes nor inhibits religion. We need to know about religion, not just ours, but all peoples'. School can and should teach the basics, leaving the questions of belief and worship to activities outside of school. Such teaching would help us to learn, and to listen.

Return to Liberty's First Principles

This debate about religion is really a debate about trust. Can we trust each person to follow his or her own spiritual journey? Can we trust the wisdom of respecting differences and dissent? The philosophy of freedom is not the elixir of all life. It does not satisfy the spiritual quest, should we choose to make one, but it is the essential vehicle which makes that spiritual quest possible. Liberty for one, as Martin Luther King, Jr. reminds us, necessarily means liberty for all.

Just because we are feeling morally adrift in today's society doesn't mean we have license to abandon our first principles. Many of our historical wounds have been self-inflicted: slavery, the mistreatment of Native Americans, the internment of Japanese Americans during World War II, the cowardice of the McCarthy communist witch-hunt and the nation's willingness to allow it. Because our multiple follies are repeated—the lessons of history being soon forgotten or imperfectly learned—our political salvation is in protection of individual conscience, individual empowerment and the infinite chance that those give us to do better, to try again and again and again.

Collectively, we recognize that we are all in this life, in this government and in this society together. Individually, we recognize that we may differ wildly on issues of ultimate concern. The collective pursuit of happiness depends on respect for the individual's right to pursue the life of the spirit actively or not at all. If we miss that point, we miss the point of the First Amendment and the spirit of liberty. As Thomas Jefferson said: "It does me no injury for my neighbor to say there are twenty gods or no god. It neither picks my pocket nor breaks my leg."

A Christian Nation

In the fall of 1993 Governor Kirk Fordice of Mississippi declared that we are a Christian nation. When one of his fellow Republican governors asked if he didn't mean a Judeo-Christian nation, he snapped back that, if he had meant that, he would have said it. Many agree, and cite our coinage, which bears the inscription, "In God We Trust," or our Pledge of Allegiance, which describes us as "one nation under God." They point to chaplains in the military, the prayers that open Congress, and the words of the Declaration of Independence that invoke God's blessing.

What does it mean to say we are a Christian nation? One can only guess at Governor Fordice's definition, but if he was referring merely to a majority of Americans who profess to practice Christianity, he may be correct. If he was suggesting that those who practice faiths other than Christianity are second-class citizens in this country, or that America is divinely blessed above other nations, or that our government should operate on Christian religious principles, then he needs a civics lesson. Not only does the First Amendment strictly prohibit government-endorsed religion, but it protects the conscience which acknowledges no religion. That question is so personal as to brook no governmental intrusion. Moreover, Article VI of the Constitution prohibits any religious test for qualification to any office of public trust in the U.S. Government and, through the Fourteenth Amendment, that prohibition applies to all state and local governments as well.

Laws against blasphemy cannot be passed, since both the establishment and free exercise clauses of the First Amendment prohibit them. How could the government, without endorsing a religion, determine what its tenets were to such a degree that it could draft a statute prohibiting attack on those tenets? And if free conscience is protected, how could one be prosecuted for attacking a religion believed to be untrue?

The point again is respect, respect for those who are not of the majority, as well as for those who are. Granted, the Declaration of Independence talks about laws of nature and nature's God, and invokes repeatedly God's blessing and judgment upon the launching of a new nation, but that does not invite the mixing of religion and government. Jefferson, who wrote the Declaration of Independence, was unequivocal about the necessity for separation. Madison, whose views were equally unequivocal, provided much of the language for the First Amendment.

In the spring of each year, high school seniors plan their graduation. It is a significant event, a rite of passage, a somewhat scary farewell to childhood and acknowledgment of the duties of adulthood. It is a big event in the students' lives, and many would like to invite God's attention through public prayers and invocations. Indeed, the Christian Coalition and others, either through threatened law suits or self-help promotions for students, seek to assist such student desires. The fervor with which students pursue their desire to pray within a school-sanctioned event demonstrates our schools' failure adequately to have taught the First Amendment.

The First Amendment works only if it protects everybody. Prayer at a public school graduation is not a matter of the majority's will. It is subject to the right of each student to be free from coercion. That Congress should pass no law respecting an establishment of religion means exactly that. That each individual should have free conscience to pray or not to pray means exactly that. And those two imperatives, taken together, compel the conclusion that public prayers, be they student-inspired, student-led, administration-inspired or administration-led, are out of bounds—not only because the U.S. Supreme Court says so, but because our most fundamental beliefs as Americans say so.

Questions for Discussion

1. *Begin the discussion of this chapter by reviewing a topic that was especially controversial. Use the technique of attentive listening followed by stating an opposing viewpoint as on page 60.*

2. *Brainstorm examples of how less crime and better morality could be promoted without resorting to school prayer. Use the newspaper and periodicals to find current examples.*

3. *Have you ever been forced to participate in a religion or religious practice against your will? Is this ever justifiable? If so, when?*

4. *Suppose a religion favors controversial practices such as smoking peyote or sacrificing animals. Should the state interfere?*

5. *Research project: Cite examples from newspapers and periodicals of religious persecution. Discuss the government's role.*

6. *Is it inconsistent that the framers of the Declaration of Independence should call for god's protection of this new country and yet, in the First Amendment, separate religion and politics? Why or why not?*

7. *Do you agree with Madison's arguments against teaching Protestant religion in school? What counterarguments can one make?*

8. *Discuss the issue of trust as it relates to your daily life. Must trust be earned or is it a right? How would your day be different if you were extended unlimited trust (to go to school, to do your school work, to fulfill your job, to do your chores, and so forth)? Could society function successfully if everyone was reared on unlimited trust?*

9. *After using any or all of the preceeding questions and activities, repeat the listening process using a topic that generated heated discussion. Ask students to assess the effect the listening exercise had on their understanding of the controversy and their position.*

Sources

Alley, Robert S., ed. *The Founding Fathers and the Courage to Doubt.* Buffalo, N.Y.: Prometheus Press, 1985.

Alley, Robert S. *The Supreme Court on Church and State.* New York: Oxford University Press, 1988.

Bates, Stephen. *Battleground.* New York: Poseidon Press, 1993.

Davis, Derek. *Original Intent.* Buffalo, N.Y.: Prometheus Books, 1991.

Hunter, James Davidson, and Oz Guinness, eds. *Articles of Faith, Articles of Peace.* Washington, D.C.: The Brookings Institution, 1990.

---

[1]Daniel Boorstin, "The Founding Fathers and the Courage to Doubt" in Robert S. Alley, ed., *James Madison on Religious Liberty* (Buffalo: Prometheus Books, 1985), p. 214.

Chapter Five

OUR TROUBLED HISTORY OF REUNION

OUR SYSTEM HAS BUILT within it the tools of self-criticism, correction and amendment. It contemplates citizens who are both flawed and noble, and capable of injustice and self-criticism. It is an earthquake-proof bridge, designed to withstand tremors and quakes and to remain standing, open for social commerce, so long as its citizens remain involved.

In public ethics we struggle between competing values of union and separation, dependence and independence, community and individuality. We recognize that while government must exist on majoritarian principles, the will of the majority is not always the equivalent of the common good. The common good is and always will be that every individual has free conscience, spiritual choice and the right to criticize the government openly, forthrightly, brutally. When we recognize that the pursuit of happiness is both collective and individual, then we see that justice is our responsibility, not that of some impersonal system.

This is not to suggest that within our first principles of freedom, equality, free expression and free spirit are all of the individual and collective beliefs that would make up an ethical system. The church, the family, our education and innumerable other sources can help guide us in defining sins and virtues. What is critical about the ethical substance of the American system of government is that it makes such a quest possible. Freedom is chaotic and depends, as Madison said in *Federalist No. 55*, on a belief that democracy calls forth the noble characteristics of man to a greater degree than any other form of government. Empowered citizens are noble citizens.

Words

Meaningful, expressive language is critical to maintaining democracy, and we are crippling ours. *The Los Angeles Times* recently directed its writers not to use words such as: *co-ed, mankind, mailman* and *Dutch treat*. Also out are *deaf, gypped, hillbilly, crazy, divorcee, Indian, welsher* and *white trash*. A college professor, in one of the more asinine suggestions of late, decried the use of "disseminate," since the root of the word comes from seminal and that is masculine and somehow we need to be gender-neutral in order to be politically non-offensive. What drivel. Where is the magic and majesty of our language? What has happened to our courage, our willingness to talk to each other in robust language and persuade, cajole, caress with words and seduce with the music of language? The romantic composer Johannes Brahms said, upon leaving a luncheon in Vienna, "If there is any one here whom I have failed to offend, I humbly beg his pardon." We needn't go out of our way to offend, but we must, to save ourselves and our language, learn again to speak frankly.

Toni Morrison, in accepting her Nobel Prize in literature, spoke of the beauty and power of language—"not official language or the censoring language of the state or the trick language of journalism, but language as words, with the magic they contain when they are learned by children." It is words, she said, that empower mediation, that fend off "the scariness of things with no names" and that ease the burden of oppression. Words enable us to make some sense of our existence by standing aside and narrating it.

Our language has music and rhythm and immediacy and passion. Because time is the tyrant of television, and because TV language is corseted and trussed by scripts, the free-flowing immediacy of the spoken word on television is usually lost. With it has gone much of the spice and poetry of our tongue. Rap music, in its best examples, breathes new life into words as art. While the message is sometimes raw or hateful, the energy and immediacy and authenticity give it punch and vitality. The mental aerobics of reading poetry aloud expands our consciousness of rhythm and meter, better attunes us to messages of our culture, and extends the use of metaphor—words which evoke the sensation of other words. The significance of free speech in our culture goes far beyond being able to choose which newspaper we will read. In its broadest sense, free speech is the description of life itself. It is those who have inflamed ordinary words with extraordinary meaning—Whitman and Emerson and Thoreau and Frost—who have captured the truth of our existence and have helped us as a country to better understand ourselves.

Just as we must protect the vitality and accuracy of our language, so we must also know our history as it teaches us the lessons necessary to understand our national ethic of freedom and responsibility. Two defining examples are found in Lincoln's "Gettysburg Address" and Martin Luther King, Jr.'s "Letter from Birmingham Jail." Each, written at a time of crisis, reaffirms our nation's first principles in a call to reunion, dedication and courage.

"The Gettysburg Address" and Individual Responsibility

Union victory was by no means assured as Lincoln traveled by train from Washington to Gettysburg on November 18, 1863. Four months after the battle in which 45,000 men had fallen dead or wounded, the battlefield was littered with the rotting bodies of horses, cannon-shattered trees and broken equipment. Lee had retreated, but not in defeat, and little in the military strategy of the North gave cause for optimism in the continued course of the war. The war's uncertainty added moral authority to Lincoln's words as he envisioned what should be rather than what was already ordained. His address [plate 10] was a call for three fundamentally ethical actions: cleansing, rededication and courage.

Lincoln first reminds us of the birth of our nation in liberty and equality. That a war is being fought over those principles, differently understood by brothers and neighbors, requires a true investigation of just what is meant by "liberty" and the proposition that "all men are created equal." For the war, after all, is not just for any union, but for *the union* which is dedicated to those propositions of equality and freedom. The imagery that he uses is that of birth, death and rebirth. The nation was conceived and men died so that it might live. That a nation is living means many things—that it could grow, in health or sickness, and that it could continue to live or could die. The living, he says, must assure a new birth in freedom. This optimistic message echoes Madison's *Federalist No. 55* in its assurance that we Americans can recognize our failure to adhere to first principles and correct our course. The cleansing is the return to the ideal state, to the true meaning of liberty and equality.

President Lincoln uses the words "dedicate" or "dedicated" six times in a two-minute speech. We are dedicated to the proposition that men are created equal, dedicated to the preservation of the nation, dedicated to the memory of the dead, and dedicated to the unfinished business of winning the war. Why should we be so dedicated? What is it about the human condition that gives Lincoln the belief that men would shoulder this responsibility? As American writer John

Dos Passos says, such dedication depends upon a spirit in man which strives for the good—a proposition in itself that can neither be tested nor disproved by logic or scientific experiment. Lincoln identifies a fundamental inner imperative which suggests that ethical action is intuitive if men are free and equal. Jefferson held a similar belief. He thought that an innate sense of justice in free men would hold our society together.

Finally, Lincoln evokes the courage of our founding fathers and of the brave who fought and died on the meadows and hills at Gettysburg to inspire us, the living, to continue the task. That call to courage compels us today to be midwives in another rebirth of freedom. The scarred and economically deprived streets of Washington, D.C., and New York City are our Gettysburg, and the crisis to the union is no less severe, the outcome no more certain. Lincoln knew that no generation escapes history. We are writing it with our deeds and with our defaults.

Lincoln's vision speaks to each of us no matter where we see ourselves on the political spectrum. His belief in individual responsibility and individual liberty is a profoundly conservative point of departure. His doctrine of equality and call to bold action are decidedly liberal. His vision favors neither one side nor the other but serves equally all who respond to his challenge. Every American school child used to memorize "The Gettysburg Address." None were harmed by the exercise.

"Letter from Birmingham Jail" and Individual Responsibility

Martin Luther King, Jr. was involved in a war no less hostile, no less engaging and no less universal than Lincoln's Civil War. Since the 1870s, recreational lynchings, lack of education, voting rights and economic opportunity, and denial even of the right to sit where one wanted on a bus were the daily fare of Blacks in America. The country had learned to look the other way, and so ingrained was that blindness, that only the creation of tension by nonviolent confrontation would blast us from our lethargy. Those in power, he observed, seldom give up their privileges voluntarily.

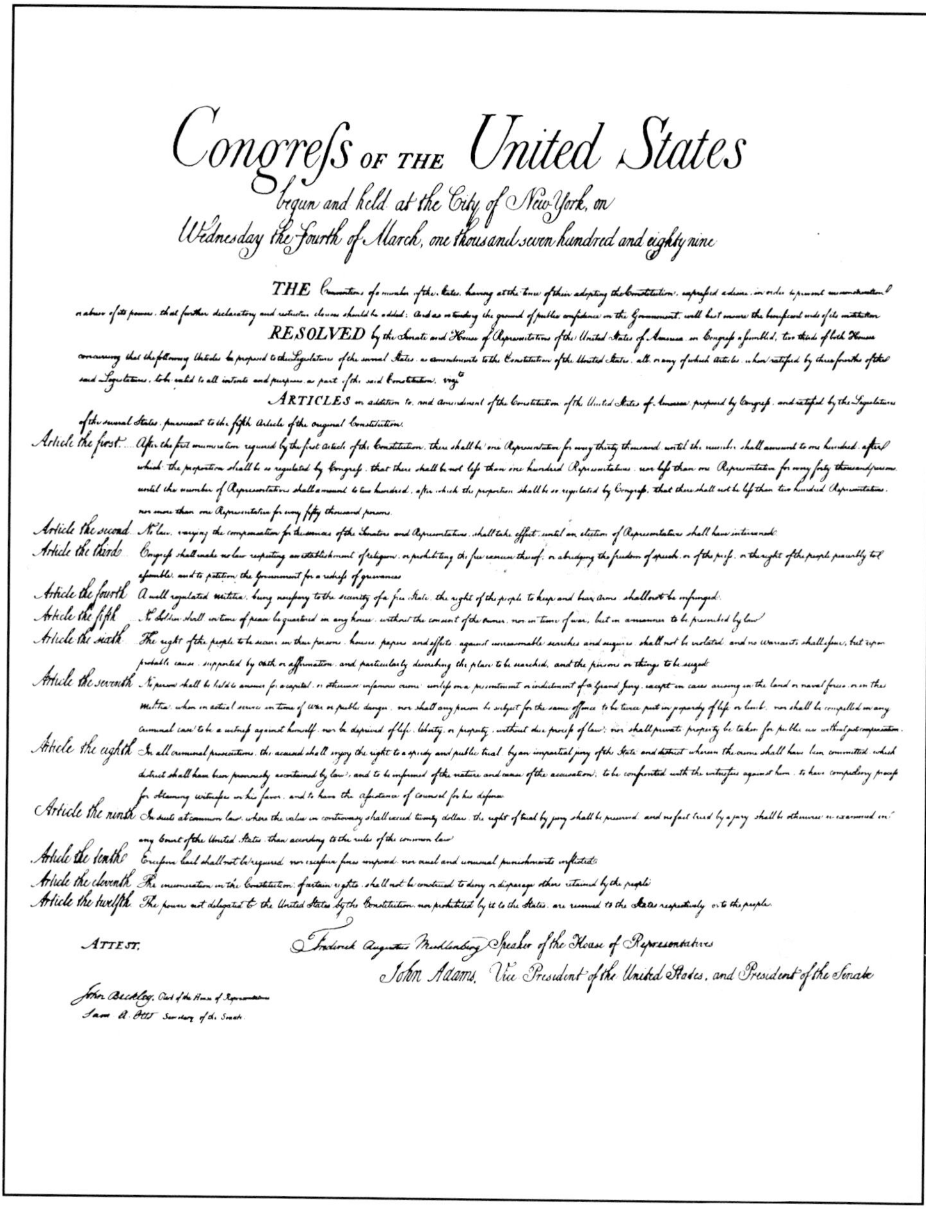

Congress of the United States

begun and held at the City of New-York, on
Wednesday the Fourth of March, one thousand seven hundred and eighty nine

THE Conventions of a number of the States, having at the time of their adopting the Constitution, expressed a desire, in order to prevent misconstruction or abuse of its powers, that further declaratory and restrictive clauses should be added: And as extending the ground of public confidence in the Government, will best ensure the beneficent ends of its institution

RESOLVED by the Senate and House of Representatives of the United States of America, in Congress assembled, two thirds of both Houses concurring, that the following Articles be proposed to the Legislatures of the several States, as amendments to the Constitution of the United States, all, or any of which Articles, when ratified by three fourths of the said Legislatures, to be valid to all intents and purposes, as part of the said Constitution; viz.

ARTICLES in addition to, and Amendment of the Constitution of the United States of America, proposed by Congress, and ratified by the Legislatures of the several States, pursuant to the fifth Article of the original Constitution.

Article the first. After the first enumeration required by the first article of the Constitution, there shall be one Representative for every thirty thousand, until the number shall amount to one hundred, after which the proportion shall be so regulated by Congress, that there shall be not less than one hundred Representatives, nor less than one Representative for every forty thousand persons, until the number of Representatives shall amount to two hundred; after which the proportion shall be so regulated by Congress, that there shall not be less than two hundred Representatives, nor more than one Representative for every fifty thousand persons.

Article the second. No law, varying the compensation for the services of the Senators and Representatives, shall take effect, until an election of Representatives shall have intervened.

Article the third. Congress shall make no law respecting an establishment of religion, or prohibiting the free exercise thereof; or abridging the freedom of speech, or of the press; or the right of the people peaceably to assemble, and to petition the Government for a redress of grievances.

Article the fourth. A well regulated militia, being necessary to the security of a free State, the right of the people to keep and bear arms, shall not be infringed.

Article the fifth. No Soldier shall, in time of peace be quartered in any house, without the consent of the owner, nor in time of war, but in a manner to be prescribed by law.

Article the sixth. The right of the people to be secure in their persons, houses, papers, and effects, against unreasonable searches and seizures, shall not be violated, and no warrants shall issue, but upon probable cause, supported by oath or affirmation, and particularly describing the place to be searched, and the persons or things to be seized.

Article the seventh. No person shall be held to answer for a capital, or otherwise infamous crime, unless on a presentment or indictment of a Grand Jury, except in cases arising in the land or naval forces, or in the Militia, when in actual service in time of War or public danger; nor shall any person be subject for the same offence to be twice put in jeopardy of life or limb; nor shall be compelled in any criminal case to be a witness against himself, nor be deprived of life, liberty, or property, without due process of law; nor shall private property be taken for public use without just compensation.

Article the eighth. In all criminal prosecutions, the accused shall enjoy the right to a speedy and public trial, by an impartial jury of the State and district wherein the crime shall have been committed, which district shall have been previously ascertained by law, and to be informed of the nature and cause of the accusation; to be confronted with the witnesses against him; to have compulsory process for obtaining witnesses in his favor, and to have the assistance of counsel for his defence.

Article the ninth. In suits at common law, where the value in controversy shall exceed twenty dollars, the right of trial by jury shall be preserved, and no fact tried by a jury shall be otherwise re-examined in any Court of the United States, than according to the rules of the common law.

Article the tenth. Excessive bail shall not be required, nor excessive fines imposed, nor cruel and unusual punishments inflicted.

Article the eleventh. The enumeration in the Constitution, of certain rights, shall not be construed to deny or disparage others retained by the people.

Article the twelfth. The powers not delegated to the United States by the Constitution, nor prohibited by it to the States, are reserved to the States respectively, or to the people.

ATTEST,

Frederick Augustus Muhlenberg Speaker of the House of Representatives
John Adams, Vice President of the United States, and President of the Senate

John Beckley, Clerk of the House of Representatives.
Sam. A. Otis Secretary of the Senate.

PLATE 1—The original *Bill of Rights*
The first two Articles failed to be ratified, making the "Article the Third" our First Amendment.

PLATE 2—Michelangelo: *Original Sin and Expulsion from Paradise*
Scala/Art Resource, NY

"SORRY, MICHELANGELO, BUT IT'S THE ONLY WAY TO GET CONGRESSIONAL FUNDING..."

PLATE 3—
Bill Schorr reprinted by
permission of UFS, Inc.

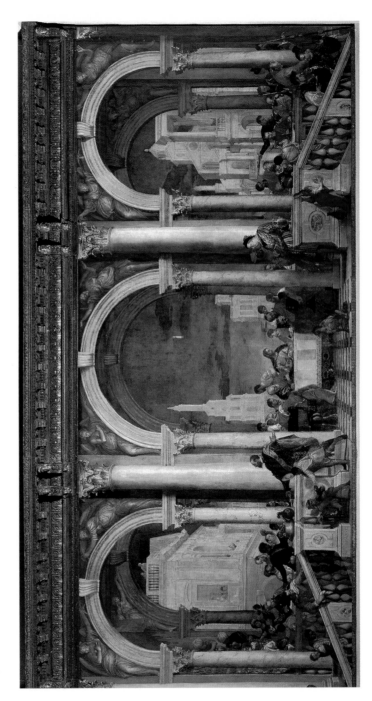

PLATE 4—Veronese: *Feast in the House of Levi*
Scala/Art Resource, NY

PLATE 5—*Aphrodite (Venus de Milo)*
Art Resource, NY

PLATE 6—Thomas Hart Benton:
Susanna and the Elders
The Fine Arts Museums
of San Francisco,
Anonymous gift, 1940.104

PLATE 7—Maria Ewing as Salome
with the severed head of John the
Baptist
Photo by Joan Marcus for
The Washington Opera.

PLATE 8—Alice Sims: *Water Babies*
Used with permission.

PLATE 9—VFW members remove the flag from the floor of the Visual Arts Center, Anchorage, Alaska.
Jim Lavrakas/Anchorage Daily News

PLATE 10—
*The Gettysburg
Address*
The Library
of Congress

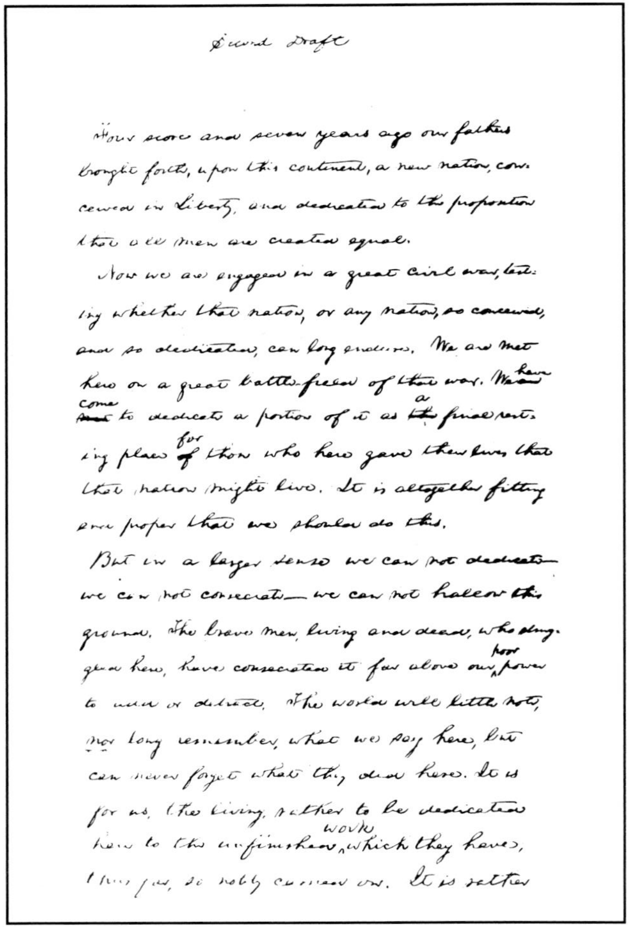

Second Draft

Four score and seven years ago our fathers brought forth, upon this continent, a new nation, conceived in liberty, and dedicated to the proposition that all men are created equal.

Now we are engaged in a great civil war, testing whether that nation, or any nation so conceived, and so dedicated, can long endure. We are met on a great battlefield of that war. We come to dedicate a portion of it, as a final resting place for those who here gave their lives that that nation might live. It is altogether fitting and proper that we should do this.

But in a larger sense we can not dedicate— we can not consecrate— we can not hallow this ground. The brave men, living and dead, who struggled here, have consecrated it far above our poor power to add or detract. The world will little note, nor long remember, what we say here, but can never forget what they did here. It is rather for us the living, rather to be dedicated here to the unfinished work which they have, thus far, so nobly carried on. It is rather

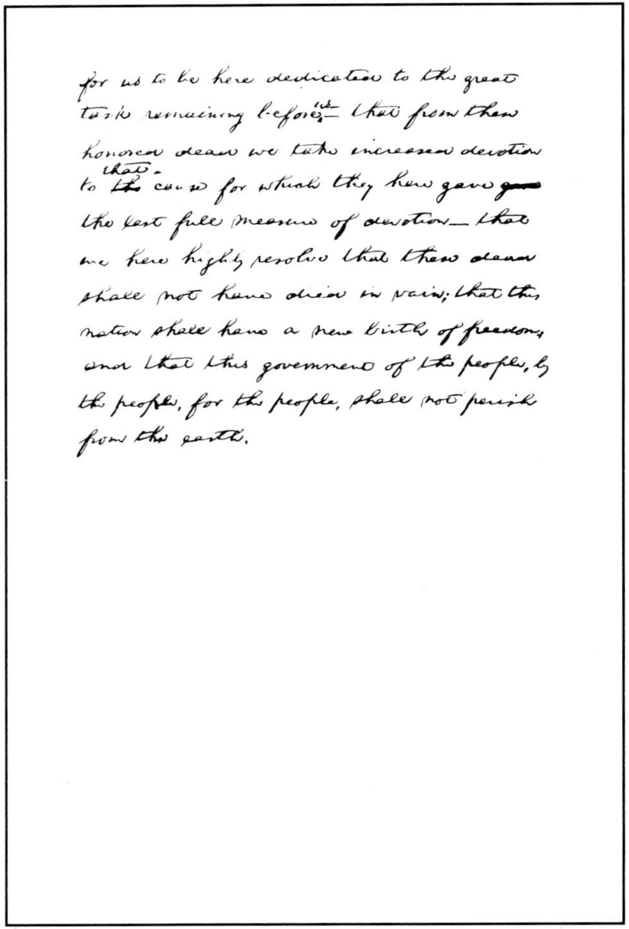

for us to be here dedicated to the great task remaining before us— that from these honored dead we take increased devotion to that cause for which they here gave the last full measure of devotion— that we here highly resolve that these dead shall not have died in vain; that this nation shall have a new birth of freedom; and that government of the people, by the people, for the people, shall not perish from the earth.

King's letter is both theoretical and practical, effective because in every sentence it seethes with moral authority. Two fundamental concepts emerge, the first being our interrelatedness and the second the necessity to return to America's first principles.

King says he is in Birmingham because injustice is there and that "injustice anywhere is a threat to justice everywhere." The battle for freedom is not just that of the Black person, but of every American citizen, and King finds the default of the supposedly moral white moderate more disturbing than the unadulterated hate of the white segregationist. The longshoreman-philosopher Eric Hoffer expressed a similar view, saying that power corrupts the few while weakness corrupts the many. Likewise, the church, says King, has failed in its moral duty. He recalls the South's beautiful churches with lofty spires and impressive buildings and asks the searing questions: "What kind of people worship here? Who is their God?" Time alone will not cure injustice. Time, he says, is neutral. Human progress depends upon human involvement, hard work and the reassertion of human dignity.

His second principle reaffirms that the birthright of all Americans is freedom. We are extremists one way or the other, either for justice or for the preservation of injustice. This message is thoroughly patriotic; King looks to America, which has been the purveyor of injustice, to reaffirm its first principles and rectify that failing. He looks to Americans to understand that it is our duty to break unjust laws (and to take the consequences) in faith that the system will right itself.

In his litany of oppressions against the Negro, he evokes the ethical strength of the Declaration of Independence, which catalogued a similar litany of offenses against King George III. He evokes the self-evident rights of life, liberty and the pursuit of happiness (by implication here, and explicitly in his "I have a dream ..." speech four months later). He talks of the deafness of those who have not heard injustice and invites divine scrutiny of his actions (as did the Declaration of Independence). He speaks of moral law, just as the Declaration of Independence talks of the "Laws of Nature" and of "Nature's God." Any law which degrades human personality is unjust. Any law which

71

compels a minority to obey but excepts the majority is unjust, and any law which is inflicted upon those who have no part in voting is unjust. One who lovingly and openly accepts the penalty for an unjust law in order to arouse the conscience of the community is, in effect, expressing the highest respect for the law. The reawakening of conscience over injustice is a step toward bringing America back "to the great wells of democracy."

King's reference to the Declaration of Independence is not accidental. He seeks revolution. He seeks morality. He seeks preservation of the union no less than Lincoln, and creation of a just society no less than Jefferson or Madison. He knows that for a healthy union to exist, justice must prevail, and that America can heal itself within its own legal and moral parameters. See Appendix IV for this remarkable treatise on morality and politics. Read it, ponder it, think how you would have acted then—and how you are acting now.

Capacity and Responsibility

"I'm too busy with my schoolwork or my job or my family to deal with all of these issues, and besides, I can't do anything about them anyway. I'm an insignificant fly in the jungle of history." It's a common response. But it's an abdication of life, not a reaffirmation of it. None of us has earned the luxury of deciding not to decide; none of us is the owner of the easy life. Even the simple expedient of thinking of our government in ethical terms is a huge step in recapturing a sense of control. From this vantage point, we view government with a completely different set of expectations. The common good, straight talk, clear objectives and a means of self-evaluation are a few immediate benefits.

The creed of the founding fathers, as is written in both the Declaration of Independence and the First Amendment, embraces an obligation to our own nation, to other nations and to posterity. Those were audacious thoughts for a country so new and so weak. But for us today this philosophy is even more profound, for we will be judged not by what we take from this world, but by what we leave. Getting our own, just for ourselves, can't be consistent with our obligations to the rest of the world and to the world's children. The founding fathers' philosophy concerned all things: life, freedom, civilization, nature and human dignity.

Our limited capacity may require us to concentrate on certain issues of most interest to us, but limited capacity is no excuse for disengagement. As Martin Luther King, Jr. points out so eloquently, we are all joined in the pursuit of justice and our success is collective. Independence leads not to self-sufficiency, but rather to codependence. Ethics beckons, nudges, encourages or nags us but is voiceless to compel us. It depends upon our willingness to be engaged rather than isolated. Ethics poses two equally important questions: How do I go about making a decision, and how do I justify that decision to others? Our first principles help us in making decisions, and our accountability helps us to justify those decisions to others. Thus, accountability in a democracy is required not only of our leaders, but of each of us in our continual evaluation of how we are living the privilege of citizenship.

Many people carry a card in their purse or wallet that gives the steps for CPR. Should a crisis arise, they hope the card will help them save a life. A similar card for dealing with First Amendment issues (and thereby acting ethically as a citizen) might look like this:

1. Have I honestly and impartially gathered the facts?
2. Is a government agency involved?
3. Am I protecting the speaker?
4. In analyzing my response, have I put aside my own beliefs enough to respect the right of another, with whom I disagree, to be heard?
5. Is what the government is doing neutral toward religion?
6. Is what the government is doing neutral toward people associating with one another?

A similar card for our ethical first principles would ask whether a given action (or inaction) promotes equality, life, liberty and our collective happiness. If you rely only on this card, and do not continue to think and grow as a citizen, it and you will get a bit tattered around the corners. Chances are, you will use it less and less. But perhaps it will serve as a reminder of how difficult it is to live within our own noble aspirations.

The words of the poet Sam Hazo speak to all of us:

> I wish you what I wish
> myself: hard questions
> and the nights to answer them,
> the grace of disappointment,
> and the right to seem the fool
> for justice. That's enough.
> Cowards might ask for more.
> Heroes have died for less.[1]

Questions for Discussion

1. The Declaration of Independence says that among the unalienable rights are life, liberty and the pursuit of happiness. What other rights would you name? What does unalienable mean? What about economic equality?

2. If you asked a newspaper editor to define "the word," what do you think would be the response?

3. What does King mean when he says openly and lovingly breaking an unjust law shows the highest respect for the law? Do you agree? Cite examples.

4. Compare what Lincoln and King said.

5. Using the themes expressed in "The Gettysburg Address" and "Letter from Birmingham Jail," write your own version addressing the problems of violence in American society, pollution of the oceans, or world population.

6. Write rap lyrics, a poem or a song that describes your understanding of America's first principles.

7. If you were going to start a new country, what would you deem important? State-controlled resource protection? Being a good neighbor?

8. What evidence is there that men strive for "the good" in government?

9. How can people be encouraged to become more involved in government? What benefits or burdens would derive from increased involvement? Should the government have a 900 number so everyone could give an opinion on everything?

10. What First Amendment issues have come up in your school in the last year?

Sources

Boorstin, Daniel J. *The Lost World of Thomas Jefferson*. Chicago: The University of Chicago Press, 1948, 1993.

Commager, Henry Steele. *Commager on Tocqueville*. Columbia, Mo.: University of Missouri Press, 1993.

King, Martin Luther, Jr. *Letter From Birmingham Jail*. Atlanta: The King Center, 1963.

Nevins, Allen, ed. *Lincoln and The Gettysburg Address, Commemorative Papers*. Urbana: University of Illinois Press, 1964.

---

[1] Samuel Hazo, "To A Commencement of Scoundrels," *Thank A Bored Angel* (New York: New Directions, 1983), p. 29.

EPILOGUE

Books are personal statements. At least, this one is. Some believe that a book that takes a position (as opposed to merely stating both sides and letting the student choose) is unacceptable as a text. Perhaps. But a word of personal history will explain the evolution of my thoughts.

My academic degrees are in American history, Christian ethics and law. For 17 years I was a trial lawyer, with about 20 percent of my practice in the First Amendment area. I was a First Amendment moderate. That is, I argued for access of newspapers to government records and against laws that would "chill" free press or free expression. The First Amendment was one legal tool among many others to be used in service of my clients.

Then, in the summer of 1989, President Bush appointed me chairman of the National Endowment for the Arts. I was thrilled. No position, in or out of government, held as much potential to enrich people's lives. Music, poetry, dance and theater could open new vistas to schoolchildren, and we all could better understand each other through the windows that art provides into the foibles and glories of human beings.

Instead, the job was a nightmare. I was caught between the uncompromising forces who, on the one hand, saw the Arts Endowment as promoting obscenity and nonmajoritarian values and, on the other, condemned it for capitulating to censorship and artistic repression. I sought the middle ground and was creamed by both sides.

The conflict changed my life. I decided that free speech is not a compromisable issue; that if we as Americans stand for anything, it is the fierce protection of individual conscience; and that art that is offensive to some is the price of doing business. In short, I became a First Amendment radical.

After I was fired by President Bush, paradoxically I became even more dedicated to helping America reclaim its birthright of freedom. I am indebted to The Freedom Forum First Amendment Center at Vanderbilt University for giving me the time, and often the inspiration, to translate these thoughts into making the first edition of this book.

The First Amendment has allowed the creation of a unique and wonderful cultural ecology in the United States. Our history is written as much by poets and singers as by presidents and generals. We learn more about life through reading the thoughts of long-dead authors than we do by listening to politicians and judges. Politics demands our day-to-day attention, but art teaches us the lasting lessons of humility, gentility, love and wisdom.

To be locked out of the appreciation of rhythm and harmony or the nuance and beauty of dance is as numbing and dehumanizing as being unable to read. Our search for compassion for our fellow citizens and the citizens of the world will be more successful if we command the language and vision of the arts.

My personal journey leads me to believe that the arts are a vital component of the free spirit that our First Amendment so jealously guards. As contentious and chartless as our present social and political life seems to be, I believe, with Madison and Jefferson, that an innate sense of justice binds us together as a society. Art gives form to that invisible truth.

Appendices

The Declaration of Independence

In Congress July 4, 1776.
The unanimous Declaration of
the thirteen united States of America,

WHEN IN THE COURSE of human events, it becomes necessary for one people to dissolve the political bands which have connected them with another, and to assume among the powers of the earth, the separate and equal station to which the Laws of Nature and of Nature's God entitle them, a decent respect to the opinions of mankind requires that they should declare the causes which impel them to the separation.—

We hold these truths to be self-evident, that all men are created equal, that they are endowed by their Creator with certain unalienable Rights, that among these are Life, Liberty, and the pursuit of

Happiness. That to secure these rights, Governments are instituted among Men, deriving their just powers from the consent of the governed,—That whenever any Form of Government becomes destructive of these ends, it is the Right of the People to alter or to abolish it, and to institute new Government, laying its foundation on such principles and organizing its powers in such form, as to them shall seem most likely to effect their Safety and Happiness. Prudence, indeed, will dictate that Governments long established should not be changed for light and transient causes; and accordingly all experience hath shewn, that mankind are more disposed to suffer, while evils are sufferable, than to right themselves by abolishing the forms to which they are accustomed. But when a long train of abuses and usurpations, pursuing invariably the same Object evinces a design to reduce them under absolute Despotism, it is their right, it is their duty, to throw off such Government, and to provide new Guards for their future security.—Such has been the patient sufferance of these Colonies; and such is now the necessity which constrains them to alter their former Systems of Government. The history of the present King of Great Britain is a history of repeated injuries and usurpations, all having in direct object the establishment of an absolute Tyranny over these States. To prove this, let Facts be submitted to a candid world.—

He has refused his Assent to Laws, the most wholesome and necessary for the public good.—

He has forbidden his Governors to pass Laws of immediate and pressing importance, unless suspended in their operation till his Assent should be obtained; and when so suspended, has utterly neglected to attend to them.—

He has refused to pass other Laws for the accommodation of large districts of people, unless those people would relinquish the right of Representation in the Legislature, a right inestimable to them and formidable to tyrants only.—

He has called together legislative bodies at places unusual, uncomfortable, and distant from the depository of their public Records, for the sole purpose of fatiguing them into compliance with his measures.—

He has dissolved Representative Houses repeatedly, for opposing with manly firmness his invasions on the rights of the people.—

He has refused for a long time, after such dissolutions, to cause others to be elected; whereby the Legislative Powers, incapable of Annihilation, have returned to the People at large for their exercise; the State remaining in the mean time exposed to all the dangers of invasion from without, and convulsions within.—

He has endeavored to prevent the population of these States; for that purpose obstructing the Laws for Naturalization of Foreigners; refusing to pass others to encourage their migration hither, and raising the conditions of new Appropriations of Lands.—

He has obstructed the Administration of Justice, by refusing his Assent to Laws for establishing Judiciary Powers.—

He has made Judges dependent on his Will alone, for the tenure of their offices, and the amount and payment of their salaries.—

He has erected a multitude of New Offices, and sent hither swarms of Officers to harass our people, and eat out their substance.—

He has kept among us, in times of peace, Standing Armies without the Consent of our legislatures.—

He has affected to render the Military independent of and superior to the Civil Power.—

He has combined with others to subject us to a jurisdiction foreign to our constitution, and unacknowledged by our laws; giving his Assent to their acts of pretended legislation:—

For quartering large bodies of armed troops among us:—

For protecting them, by a mock Trial, from Punishment for any Murders which they should commit on the Inhabitants of these States:—

For cutting off our Trade with all parts of the world:—

For imposing Taxes on us without our Consent:—

For depriving us in many cases, of the benefits of Trial by Jury:—

For transporting us beyond Seas to be tried for pretended offences:—

For abolishing the free System of English Laws in a neighbouring Province, establishing therein an Arbitrary government, and enlarging its Boundaries so as to render it at once an example and fit instrument for introducing the same absolute rule into these Colonies:—

For taking away our Charters, abolishing our most valuable Laws, and altering fundamentally, the Forms of our Governments:—

For suspending our own Legislatures, and declaring themselves invested with power to legislate for us in all cases whatsoever.—

He has abdicated Government here, by declaring us out of his Protection and waging War against us.—

He has plundered our seas, ravaged our Coasts, burnt our towns, and destroyed the lives of our people.—

He is at this time transporting large Armies of foreign Mercenaries to compleat the works of death, desolation and tyranny, already begun with circumstances of Cruelty & perfidy scarcely paralleled in the most barbarous ages, and totally unworthy the Head of a civilized nation.—

He has constrained our fellow Citizens taken Captive on the high Seas to bear Arms against their Country, to become the executioners of their friends and Brethren, or to fall themselves by their Hands.—

He has excited domestic insurrections amongst us, and has endeavored to bring on the inhabitants of our frontiers, the merciless Indian Savages, whose known rule of warfare, is an undistinguished destruction of all ages, sexes and conditions.

In every stage of these Oppressions We have Petitioned for Redress in the most humble terms: Our repeated Petitions have been answered only by repeated injury. A Prince, whose character is thus marked by every act which may define a Tyrant, is unfit to be the ruler of a free people.

Nor have We been wanting in attentions to our Brittish brethren. We have warned them from time to time of attempts by their legislature to extend an unwarrantable jurisdiction over us. We have reminded them of the circumstances of our emigration and settlement here. We have appealed to their native justice and magnanimity, and we have conjured them by the ties of our common kindred to disavow these usurpations, which, would inevitably interrupt our connections and correspondence. They too have been deaf to the voice of justice and of consanguinity. We must, therefore, acquiesce in the necessity, which denounces our Separation, and hold them, as we hold the rest of mankind, Enemies in War, in Peace Friends.—

We, therefore, the Representatives of the united States of America, in General Congress, Assembled, appealing to the Supreme Judge of the world for the rectitude of our intentions, do, in the Name, and by Authority of the good People of these Colonies, solemnly publish and declare, That these United Colonies are, and of Right ought to be Free and Independent States; that they are Absolved from all Allegiance to the British Crown, and that all political connection between them and the State of Great Britain, is and ought to be totally dissolved; and that as Free and Independent States, they have full Power to levy War, conclude Peace, contract Alliances, establish Commerce, and to do all other Acts and Things which Independent States may of right do.—

And for the support of this Declaration, with a firm reliance on the protection of divine Providence, we mutually pledge to each other our Lives, our Fortunes and our sacred Honor.

—John Hancock, *President* [1]
—Charles Thomson, *Secretary*

New Hampshire
Josiah Barlett
Wm. Whipple
Matthew Thornton

Rhode Island
Step. Hopkins
William Ellery

Connecticut
Roger Sherman
Sam'el Huntington
Wm. Williams
Oliver Wolcott

New York
Wm. Floyd
Phil. Livingston
Frans. Lewis
Lewis Morris

New Jersey
Richd. Stockton
Jno. Witherspoon
Fras. Hopkinson
John Hart
Abra. Clark

Pennsylvania
Robt. Morris
Benjamin Rush
Benja. Franklin
John Morton
Geo. Clymer
Jas. Smith

Geo. Taylor
James Wilson
Geo. Ross

Massachusetts–Bay
Saml. Adams
John Adams
Robt. Treat Paine
Elbridge Gerry

Delaware
Caesar Rodney
Geo. Read
Tho. M'Kean

Maryland
Samuel Chase
Wm. Paca
Thos. Stone
Charles Carroll of Carrollton

Virginia
George Wythe
Richard Henry Lee
Th. Jefferson
Benja. Harrison
Thos. Nelson, jr.
Francis Lightfoot Lee
Carter Braxton

North Carolina
Wm. Hooper
Joseph Hewes
John Penn

South Carolina
Edward Rutledge
Thos. Heyward, Junr.
Thomas Lynch, Junr.
Arthur Middleton

Georgia
Button Gwinnett
Lyman Hall
Geo. Walton

---

[1] Titles of presiding officers and state names do not appear on the original document; they have been added for clarity.

Appendix II

THE CONSTITUTION OF THE UNITED STATES

Preamble

WE THE PEOPLE of the United States, in Order to form a more perfect Union, establish Justice, insure domestic Tranquility, provide for the common defence, promote the general Welfare, and secure the Blessings of Liberty to ourselves and our Posterity, do ordain and establish this Constitution for the United States of America.

Article I

Section 1. All legislative Powers herein granted shall be vested in a Congress of the United States, which shall consist of a Senate and House of Representatives.

Section 2. The House of Representatives shall be composed of Members chosen every second Year by the People of the several States, and the Electors in each State shall have the Qualifications requisite for Electors of the most numerous Branch of the State Legislature.

No Person shall be a Representative who shall not have attained to the Age of twenty five Years, and been seven Years a Citizen of the United States, and who shall not, when elected, be an Inhabitant of that State in which he shall be chosen.

Representatives and direct Taxes shall be apportioned among the several States which may be included within this Union, according to their respective Numbers, which shall be determined by adding to the whole Number of free Persons, including those bound to Service for a Term of Years, and excluding Indians not taxed, three fifths of all other Persons. The actual Enumeration shall be made within three Years after the first Meeting of the Congress of the United States, and within every subsequent Term of ten Years, in such Manner as they shall by Law direct. The Number of Representatives shall not exceed one for every thirty Thousand, but each State shall have at Least one Representative; and until such enumeration shall be made, the State of New Hampshire shall be entitled to choose three, Massachusetts eight, Rhode-Island and Providence Plantations one, Connecticut five, New-York six, New Jersey four, Pennsylvania eight, Delaware one, Maryland six, Virginia ten, North Carolina five, South Carolina five, and Georgia three.

When vacancies happen in the Representation from any State, the Executive Authority thereof shall issue Writs of Election to fill such Vacancies.

The House of Representatives shall choose their speaker and other Officers; and shall have the sole Power of Impeachment.

Section 3. The Senate of the United States shall be composed of two Senators from each State, chosen by the Legislature thereof, for six Years; and each Senator shall have one Vote.

Immediately after they shall be assembled in Consequence of the first Election, they shall be divided as equally as may be into three

Classes. The Seats of the Senators of the first Class shall be vacated at the Expiration of the second Year, of the second Class at the Expiration of the fourth Year, and of the third Class at the Expiration of the sixth Year, so that one third may be chosen every second Year; and if Vacancies happen by Resignation, or otherwise, during the Recess of the Legislature of any State, the Executive thereof may make temporary Appointments until the next Meeting of the Legislature, which shall then fill such Vacancies.

No Person shall be a Senator who shall not have attained to the Age of thirty Years, and been nine Years a Citizen of the United States, and who shall not, when elected, be an Inhabitant of that State for which he shall be chosen.

The Vice President of the United States shall be President of the Senate, but shall have no Vote, unless they be equally divided.

The Senate shall choose their other Officers, and also a President *pro tempore*, in the Absence of the Vice President, or when he shall exercise the Office of President of the United States.

The Senate shall have the sole Power to try all Impeachments. When sitting for that Purpose, they shall be on Oath or Affirmation. When the President of the United States is tried, the Chief Justice shall preside: And no Person shall be convicted without the Concurrence of two thirds of the Members present.

Judgment in Cases of Impeachment shall not extend further than to removal from Office, and disqualification to hold and enjoy any Office of honor, Trust or Profit under the United States: but the Party convicted shall nevertheless be liable and subject to Indictment, Trial, Judgment and Punishment, according to law.

Section 4. The Times, Places, and Manner of holding Elections for Senators and Representatives, shall be prescribed in each State by the Legislature thereof; but the Congress may at any time by Law make or alter such Regulations, except as to the Places of choosing Senators.

The Congress shall assemble at least once in every Year, and such Meeting shall be on the first Monday in December, unless they shall by Law appoint a different Day.

Section 5. Each House shall be the Judge of the Elections, Returns, and Qualifications of its own Members, and a Majority of each shall constitute a Quorum to do Business; but a smaller Number may adjourn from day to day, and may be authorized to compel the Attendance of absent Members, in such Manner, and under such Penalties as each House may provide.

Each House may determine the Rules of its Proceedings, punish its Members for disorderly Behaviour, and, with the Concurrence of two thirds, expel a Member.

Each House shall keep a Journal of its Proceedings, and from time to time publish the same, excepting such Parts as may in their Judgment require Secrecy; and the Yeas and Nays of the Members of either House on any question shall, at the Desire of one fifth of those Present, be entered on the Journal.

Neither House, during the Session of Congress, shall, without the Consent of the other, adjourn for more than three days, nor to any other Place than that in which the two Houses shall be sitting.

Section 6. The Senators and Representatives shall receive a Compensation for their Services, to be ascertained by Law, and paid out of the Treasury of the United States. They shall in all Cases, except Treason, Felony and Breach of the Peace, be privileged from Arrest during their Attendance at the Session of their respective Houses, and in going to and returning from the same; and for any Speech or Debate in either House, they shall not be questioned in any other Place.

No Senator or Representative shall, during the Time for which he was elected, be appointed to any civil Office under the Authority of the United States, which shall have been created, or the Emoluments whereof shall have been increased during such time; and no Person holding any Office under the United States, shall be a Member of either House during his Continuance in Office.

Section 7. All Bills for raising Revenue shall originate in the House of Representatives; but the Senate may propose or concur with Amendments as on other Bills.

Every Bill which shall have passed the House of Representatives and the Senate, shall, before it become a Law, be presented to the President of the United States; If he approve he shall sign it, but if not he shall return it, with his Objections to that House in which it shall have originated, who shall enter the Objections at large on their Journal, and proceed to reconsider it. If after such Reconsideration two thirds of that House shall agree to pass the Bill, it shall be sent, together with the Objections, to the other House, by which it shall likewise be reconsidered, and if approved by two thirds of that House, it shall become a Law. But in all such Cases the Votes of both Houses shall be determined by Yeas and Nays, and the Names of the Persons voting for and against the Bill shall be entered on the Journal of each House respectively. If any Bill shall not be returned by the President within ten Days (Sundays excepted) after it shall have been presented to him, the Same shall be a Law, in like Manner as if he had signed it, unless the Congress by their Adjournment prevent its Return, in which Case it shall not be a Law.

Every Order, Resolution, or Vote to which the Concurrence of the Senate and House of Representatives may be necessary (except on a question of Adjournment) shall be presented to the President of the United States; and before the Same shall take Effect, shall be approved by him, or being disapproved by him, shall be repassed by two thirds of the Senate and House of Representatives, according to the Rules and Limitations prescribed in the Case of a Bill.

Section 8. The Congress shall have Power To lay and collect Taxes, Duties, Imposts and Excises, to pay the Debts and provide for the common Defence and general Welfare of the United States; but all Duties, Imposts and Excises shall be uniform throughout the United States;

To borrow Money on the credit of the United States;

To regulate Commerce with foreign Nations, and among the several States, and with the Indian Tribes;

To establish an uniform Rule of Naturalization, and uniform Laws on the subject of Bankruptcies throughout the United States;

To coin Money, regulate the Value thereof, and of foreign Coin, and fix the Standard of Weights and Measures;

To provide for the Punishment of counterfeiting the Securities and current Coin of the United States;

To establish Post Offices and post Roads;

To promote the Progress of Science and useful Arts, by securing for limited Times to Authors and Inventors the exclusive Right to their respective Writings and Discoveries;

To constitute Tribunals inferior to the supreme Court;

To define and punish Piracies and Felonies committed on the high Seas, and Offences against the Law of Nations;

To declare War, grant Letters of Marque and Reprisal, and make Rules concerning Captures on Land and Water;

To raise and support Armies, but no Appropriation of Money to that Use shall be for a longer Term than two Years;

To provide and maintain a Navy;

To make Rules for the Government and Regulation of the land and naval Forces;

To provide for calling forth the Militia to execute the Laws of the Union, suppress Insurrections and repel Invasions;

To provide for organizing, arming, and disciplining, the Militia, and for governing such Part of them as may be employed in the Service of the United States, reserving to the States respectively, the Appointment of the Officers, and the Authority of training the Militia according to the discipline prescribed by Congress;

To exercise exclusive Legislation in all Cases whatsoever, over such District (not exceeding ten Miles square) as may, by Cession of particular States, and the Acceptance of Congress, become the Seat of the Government of the United States, and to exercise like Authority over all Places purchased by the Consent of the Legislature of the State in which the Same shall be, for the Erection of Forts, Magazines, Arsenals, dock-Yards, and other needful Buildings;—And

To make all Laws which shall be necessary and proper for carrying into Execution the foregoing Powers, and all other Powers vested by this Constitution in the Government of the United States, or in any Department or Officer thereof.

Section 9. The Migration or Importation of such Persons as any of the States now existing shall think proper to admit, shall not be prohibited by the Congress prior to the Year one thousand eight hundred and eight, but a Tax or duty may be imposed on such Importation, not exceeding ten dollars for each Person.

The Privilege of the Writ of *Habeas Corpus* shall not be suspended, unless when in Cases of Rebellion or Invasion the public Safety may require it.

No Bill of Attainder or *ex post facto* Law shall be passed.

No Capitation, or other direct, Tax shall be laid, unless in Proportion to the Census or Enumeration herein before directed to be taken.

No Tax or Duty shall be laid on Articles exported from any State.

No Preference shall be given by any Regulation of Commerce or Revenue to the Ports of one State over those of another: nor shall Vessels bound to, or from, one State, be obliged to enter, clear, or pay Duties in another.

No money shall be drawn from the Treasury, but in Consequence of Appropriations made by Law; and a regular Statement and Account of the Receipts and Expenditures of all public Money shall be published from time to time.

No Title of Nobility shall be granted by the United States: And no Person holding any Office of Profit or Trust under them, shall, without the Consent of the Congress, accept of any present, Emolument, Office, or Title, of any kind whatever, from any King, Prince, or foreign State.

Section 10. No State shall enter into any Treaty, Alliance, or Confederation; grant Letters of Marque and Reprisal; coin Money; emit Bills of Credit; make any Thing but gold and silver Coin a Tender in Payment of Debts; pass any Bill of Attainder, *ex post facto* Law, or Law impairing the Obligation of Contracts, or grant any Title of Nobility.

No State shall, without the Consent of the Congress, lay any Imposts or Duties on Imports or Exports, except what may be absolutely necessary for executing its inspection Laws: and the net Produce of all Duties and Imposts, laid by any State on Imports or Exports, shall be for the Use of the Treasury of the United States; and all such Laws shall be subject to the Revision and Control of the Congress.

No State shall, without the Consent of the Congress, lay any Duty of Tonnage, keep Troops, or Ships of War in time of Peace, enter into any Agreement or Compact with another State, or with a foreign Power, or engage in War, unless actually invaded, or in such imminent Danger as will not admit of delay.

Article II

Section 1. The executive Power shall be vested in a President of the United States of America. He shall hold his Office during the Term of four Years, and, together with the Vice President, chosen for the same term, be elected, as follows:

Each State shall appoint, in such Manner as the Legislature thereof may direct, a Number of Electors, equal to the whole Number of Senators and Representatives to which the State may be entitled in the Congress: but no Senator or Representative, or Person holding an Office of Trust or Profit under the United States, shall be appointed an Elector.

The Electors shall meet in their respective States, and vote by Ballot for two Persons, of whom one at least shall not be an Inhabitant of the same State with themselves. And they shall make a List of all the Persons voted for, and of the Number of Votes for each; which List they shall sign and certify, and transmit sealed to the Seat of the Government of the United States, directed to the President of the Senate. The President of the Senate shall, in the Presence of the Senate and House of Representatives, open all the Certificates, and the Votes shall then be counted. The Person having the greatest Number of Votes shall be the President, if such Number be a majority of the whole Number of Electors appointed; and if there be no more than one who have such Majority, and have an equal Number of Votes, then the House of Representatives shall immediately choose by Ballot one of them for President; and if no Person have a Majority, then from the five highest on the List the said House shall in like Manner choose the

President. But in choosing the President, the Votes shall be taken by States, the Representation from each State having one Vote; A quorum for this Purpose shall consist of a Member or Members from two thirds of the States, and a Majority of all the States shall be necessary to a Choice. In every Case, after the Choice of the President, the Person having the greatest Number of Votes of the Electors shall be the Vice President. But if there should remain two or more who have equal Votes, the Senate shall choose from them by Ballot the Vice President.

The Congress may determine the Time of choosing the Electors, and the Day on which they shall give their Votes; which Day shall be the same throughout the United States.

No Person except a natural born Citizen, or a Citizen of the United States, at the time of the Adoption of this Constitution, shall be eligible to the Office of President; neither shall any Person be eligible to that Office who shall not have attained to the Age of thirty five Years, and been fourteen Years a Resident within the United States.

In Case of the Removal of the President from Office, or of his Death, Resignation, or Inability to discharge the Powers and Duties of the said Office, the Same shall devolve on the Vice President, and the Congress may by Law provide for the Case of Removal, Death, Resignation or Inability, both of the President and Vice President, declaring what Officer shall then act as President, and such Officer shall act accordingly, until the Disability be removed, or a President shall be elected.

The President shall, at stated Times, receive for his Services, a Compensation, which shall neither be increased nor diminished during the Period for which he shall have been elected, and he shall not receive within that Period any other Emolument from the United States, or any of them.

Before he enter on the Execution of his Office, he shall take the following Oath or Affirmation:—"I do solemnly swear (or affirm) that I will faithfully execute the Office of President of the United States, and will to the best of my Ability, preserve, protect and defend the Constitution of the United States."

Section 2. The President shall be Commander in Chief of the Army and Navy of the United States, and of the Militia of the several States, when called into the actual Service of the United States; he may require the Opinion, in writing, of the principal Officer in each of the executive Departments, upon any Subject relating to the Duties of their respective Offices, and he shall have Power to grant Reprieves and Pardons for Offences against the United States, except in Cases of Impeachment.

He shall have Power, by and with the Advice and Consent of the Senate, to make Treaties, provided two thirds of the Senators present concur; and he shall nominate, and by and with the Advice and Consent of the Senate, shall appoint Ambassadors, other public Ministers and Consuls, Judges of the supreme Court, and all other Officers of the United States, whose Appointments are not herein otherwise provided for, and which shall be established by Law: but the Congress may by Law vest the Appointment of such inferior Officers, as they think proper, in the President alone, in the Courts of Law, or in the Heads of Departments.

The President shall have Power to fill up all Vacancies that may happen during the Recess of the Senate, by granting Commissions which shall expire at the End of their next Session.

Section 3. He shall from time to time give to the Congress Information of the State of the Union, and recommend to their Consideration such Measures as he shall judge necessary and expedient; he may, on extraordinary Occasions, convene both Houses, or either of them, and in Case of Disagreement between them, with Respect to the Time of Adjournment, he may adjourn them to such Time as he shall think proper; he shall receive Ambassadors and other public Ministers; he shall take Care that the Laws be faithfully executed, and shall Commission all the Officers of the United States.

Section 4. The President, Vice President, and all civil Officers of the United States, shall be removed from Office on Impeachment for, and Conviction of, Treason, Bribery, or other High Crimes and Misdemeanors.

Article III

Section 1. The judicial Power of the United States, shall be vested in one supreme Court, and in such inferior Courts as the Congress may from time to time ordain and establish. The Judges, both of the supreme and inferior Courts, shall hold their Offices during good Behaviour, and shall, at stated Times, receive for their Services, a Compensation, which shall not be diminished during their Continuance in Office.

Section 2. The judicial Power shall extend to all Cases, in Law and Equity, arising under this Constitution, the Laws of the United States, and Treaties made, or which shall be made, under their Authority;— to all Cases affecting Ambassadors, other public Ministers and Consuls;—to all Cases of admiralty and maritime Jurisdiction;—to Controversies to which the United States shall be a Party;—to Controversies between two or more States; between a State and Citizens of another state;—between Citizens of different States;—between Citizens of the same State claiming Lands under Grants of different States, and between a State, or the Citizens thereof, and foreign States, Citizens or Subjects.

In all Cases affecting Ambassadors, other public Ministers and Consuls, and those in which a State shall be Party, the supreme Court shall have original Jurisdiction. In all the other Cases before mentioned, the supreme Court shall have appellate Jurisdiction, both as to Law and Fact, with such Exceptions, and under such Regulations as the Congress shall make.

The Trial of all Crimes, except in Cases of Impeachment, shall be by Jury; and such Trial shall be held in the State where the said Crimes shall have been committed; but when not committed within any State, the Trial shall be at such Place or Places as the Congress may by Law have directed.

Section 3. Treason against the United States, shall consist only in levying War against them, or in adhering to their Enemies, giving them Aid and Comfort. No Person shall be convicted of Treason unless on the Testimony of two Witnesses to the same overt Act, or on Confession in open Court.

The Congress shall have Power to declare the Punishment of Treason, but no Attainder of Treason shall work Corruption of Blood, or Forfeiture except during the Life of the Person attainted.

Article IV

Section 1. Full Faith and Credit shall be given in each State to the public Acts, Records, and judicial Proceedings of every other State. And the Congress may by general Laws prescribe the Manner in which such Acts, Records and Proceedings shall be proved, and the Effect thereof.

Section 2. The Citizens of each State shall be entitled to all Privileges and Immunities of Citizens in the several States.

A Person charged in any State with Treason, Felony, or other Crime, who shall flee from Justice, and be found in another State, shall on Demand of the executive Authority of the State from which he fled, be delivered up, to be removed to the State having Jurisdiction of the Crime.

No Person held to Service or Labour in one State, under the Laws thereof, escaping into another, shall, in Consequence of any Law or Regulation therein, be discharged from such Service or Labour, but shall be delivered up on Claim of the Party to whom such Service or Labour may be due.

Section 3. New States may be admitted by the Congress into this Union; but no new State shall be formed or erected within the Jurisdiction of any other State; nor any State be formed by the Junction of two or more States, or Parts of States, without the Consent of the Legislatures of the States concerned as well as of the Congress.

The Congress shall have Power to dispose of and make all needful Rules and Regulations respecting the Territory or other Property belonging to the United States; and nothing in this Constitution shall be so construed as to Prejudice any Claims of the United States, or of any particular State.

Section 4. The United States shall guarantee to every State in this Union a Republican Form of Government, and shall protect each of them against Invasion; and on Application of the Legislature, or of the Executive (when the Legislature cannot be convened) against domestic Violence.

Article V

The Congress, whenever two thirds of both Houses shall deem it necessary, shall propose Amendments to this Constitution, or, on the Application of the Legislatures of two thirds of the several States, shall call a Convention for proposing Amendments, which, in either Case, shall be valid to all Intents and Purposes, as Part of this Constitution, when ratified by the Legislatures of three fourths of the several States, or by Conventions in three fourths thereof, as the one or the other Mode of Ratification may be proposed by the Congress; Provided that no Amendment which may be made prior to the Year One thousand eight hundred and eight shall in any Manner affect the first and fourth Clauses in the Ninth Section of the first Article; and that no State, without its Consent, shall be deprived of its equal Suffrage in the Senate.

Article VI

All Debts contracted and Engagements entered into, before the Adoption of this Constitution, shall be as valid against the United States under this Constitution, as under the Confederation.

This Constitution, and the Laws of the United States which shall be made in Pursuance thereof; and all Treaties made, or which shall be made, under the Authority of the United States, shall be the supreme Law of the Land; and the Judges in every State shall be bound thereby, any Thing in the Constitution or Laws of any State to the Contrary notwithstanding.

The Senators and Representatives before mentioned, and the Members of the several State Legislatures, and all executive and judicial Officers, both of the United States and of the several States, shall be bound by Oath or Affirmation, to support this Constitution; but no religious Test shall ever be required as a Qualification to any Office or public Trust under the United States.

Article VII

The Ratification of the Conventions of nine States, shall be sufficient for the Establishment of this Constitution between the States so ratifying the Same.

Done in Convention by the Unanimous Consent of the States present the Seventeenth Day of September in the Year of our Lord one thousand seven hundred and Eighty seven and of the Independence of the United States of America the Twelfth. In Witness whereof we have hereunto subscribed our Names,

Geo. Washington—*President and deputy from Virginia*
Attest William Jackson—*Secretary*

New Hampshire
John Langdon
Nicholas Gilman

Massachusetts
Nathaniel Gorham
Rufus King

Connecticut
Wm. Saml. Johnson
Roger Sherman

New York
Alexander Hamilton

New Jersey
Wil. Livingston
David Brearley.
Wm. Paterson.
Jona. Dayton

Pennsylvania
B. Franklin
Thomas Mifflin
Robt. Morris
Geo. Clymer
Thos. FizSimons
Jared Ingersoll
James Wilson.
Gouv Morris

Delaware
Geo. Read
Gunning Bedford Jun
John Dickinson
Richard Bassett
Jaco. Broom

Maryland
James McHenry
Dan of St. Thos. Jenifer
Danl. Carroll

Virginia
John Blair—
James Madison Jr.

North Carolina
Wm. Blount,
Richd. Dobbs Spaight.
Hu. Williamson

South Carolina
J. Rutledge
Charles Cotesworth Pinckney
Charles Pinckney
Pierce Butler.

Georgia
William Few
Abr. Baldwin

Amendments to the Constitution

(The first ten Amendments were ratified December 15, 1791, and form what is known as the *Bill of Rights*.)

Amendment 1

Congress shall make no law respecting an establishment of religion, or prohibiting the free exercise thereof; or abridging the freedom of speech, or of the press; or the right of the people peaceably to assemble, and to petition the Government for a redress of grievances.

Amendment 2

A well regulated Militia, being necessary to the security of a free State, the right of the people to keep and bear Arms, shall not be infringed.

Amendment 3

No Soldier shall, in time of peace be quartered in any house, without the consent of the Owner, nor in time of war, but in a manner to be prescribed by law.

Amendment 4

The right of the people to be secure in their persons, houses, papers, and effects, against unreasonable searches and seizures, shall not be violated, and no warrants shall issue, but upon probable cause, supported by oath or affirmation, and particularly describing the place to be searched, and the persons or things to be seized.

Amendment 5

No person shall be held to answer for a capital, or otherwise infamous crime, unless on a presentment or indictment of a Grand Jury, except in cases arising in the land or naval forces, or in the militia, when in actual service in time of war or public danger; nor shall any person be subject for the same offence to be twice put in jeopardy of life or limb; nor shall be compelled in any criminal case to be a witness against himself, nor be deprived of life, liberty, or property, without due process of law; nor shall private property be taken for public use, without just compensation.

Amendment 6

In all criminal prosecutions, the accused shall enjoy the right to a speedy and public trial, by an impartial jury of the State and district wherein the crime shall have been committed, which district shall have been previously ascertained by law, and to be informed of the nature and cause of the accusation; to be confronted with the witnesses against him; to have compulsory process for obtaining witnesses in his favor, and to have the assistance of counsel for his defence.

Amendment 7

In Suits at common law, where the value in controversy shall exceed twenty dollars, the right of trial by jury shall be preserved, and no fact tried by a jury, shall be otherwise re-examined in any Court of the United States, than according to the rules of the common law.

Amendment 8

Excessive bail shall not be required, nor excessive fines imposed, nor cruel and unusual punishments inflicted.

Amendment 9

The enumeration in the Constitution, of certain rights, shall not be construed to deny or disparage others retained by the people.

Amendment 10

The powers not delegated to the United States by the Constitution, nor prohibited by it to the States, are reserved to the States respectively, or to the people.

Amendment 11 *(Ratified February 7, 1795)*

The Judicial power of the United States shall not be construed to extend to any suit in law or equity, commenced or prosecuted against one of the United States by Citizens of another State, or by Citizens or Subjects of any Foreign State.

Amendment 12 *(Ratified July 27, 1804)*

The Electors shall meet in their respective states and vote by ballot for President and Vice President, one of whom, at least, shall not be an inhabitant of the same state with themselves; they shall name in their ballots the person voted for as President, and in distinct ballots the person voted for as Vice President, and they shall make distinct lists of all persons voted for as President, and of all persons voted for as Vice President, and of the number of votes for each, which lists they shall sign and certify, and transmit sealed to the seat of the government of the United States, directed to the President of the Senate;—The President of the Senate shall, in the presence of the Senate and House of Representatives, open all the certificates and the votes shall then be counted;—The person having the greatest number of votes for President, shall be the President, if such number be a majority of the whole number of Electors appointed; and if no person have such majority, then from the persons having the highest numbers not exceeding three on the list of those voted for as President, the House of Representatives shall choose immediately, by ballot, the President. But in choosing the President, the votes shall be taken by states, the representation from each state having one vote; a quorum for this purpose shall consist of a member or members from two-thirds of the states, and a majority of all the states shall be necessary to a choice. And if the House of Representatives shall not choose a President whenever the right of choice shall devolve upon them, before the fourth day of March next following, then the Vice President shall act as President, as in the case of the death or other constitutional disability of the President.—The person having the greatest number of votes as Vice President, shall be the Vice President, if such number be a majority of the whole number of Electors appointed, and if no person have a majority, then from the two highest numbers on the list, the Senate shall choose the Vice President; a quorum for the purpose shall consist of two-thirds of the whole number of Senators, and a majority of the whole number shall be necessary to a choice. But no person constitutionally ineligible to the office of President shall be eligible to that of Vice President of the United States.

Amendment 13 *(Ratified December 6, 1865)*
Section 1. Neither Slavery, nor involuntary servitude, except as a punishment for crime whereof the party shall have been duly convicted, shall exist within the United States, or any place subject to their jurisdiction.

Section 2. Congress shall have power to enforce this article by appropriate legislation.

Amendment 14 *(Ratified July 9, 1868)*
Section 1. All persons born or naturalized in the United States, and subject to the jurisdiction thereof, are citizens of the United States and of the State wherein they reside. No State shall make or enforce any law which shall abridge the privileges or immunities of citizens of the United States; nor shall any State deprive any person of life, liberty, or property, without due process of law; nor deny to any person within its jurisdiction the equal protection of the laws.

Section 2. Representatives shall be apportioned among the several States according to their respective numbers, counting the whole number of persons in each State, excluding Indians not taxed. But when the right to vote at any election for the choice of electors for President and Vice President of the United States, Representatives in Congress, the Executive and Judicial officers of a State, or the members of the Legislature thereof, is denied to any of the male inhabitants of such State, being twenty-one years of age, and citizens of the United States, or in any way abridged, except for participation in rebellion, or other crime, the basis of representation therein shall be reduced in the proportion which the number of such male citizens shall bear to the whole number of male citizens twenty-one years of age in such State.

Section 3. No person shall be a Senator or Representative in Congress, or elector of President and Vice President, or hold any office, civil or military, under the United States, or under any State, who, having previously taken an oath, as a member of Congress, or as an officer of the United States, or as a member of any State legislature, or as an executive or judicial officer of any State, to support the Constitution of the United States, shall have engaged in insurrection or rebellion against the same, or given aid or comfort to the enemies thereof. But Congress may by a vote of two-thirds of each House, remove such disability.

Section 4. The validity of the public debt of the United States, authorized by law, including debts incurred for payment of pensions and bounties for services in suppressing insurrection or rebellion, shall not be questioned. But neither the United States nor any State shall assume or pay any debt or obligation incurred in aid of insurrection or rebellion against the United States, or any claim for the loss or emancipation of any slave; but all such debts, obligations and claims shall be held illegal and void.

Section 5. The Congress shall have power to enforce, by appropriate legislation, the provision of this article.

Amendment 15 *(Ratified February 3, 1870)*
Section 1. The right of citizens of the United States to vote shall not be denied or abridged by the United States or by any State on account of race, color or previous condition of servitude.

Section 2. The Congress shall have power to enforce this article by appropriate legislation.

Amendment 16 *(Ratified February 3, 1913)*

The Congress shall have power to lay and collect taxes on incomes, from whatever source derived, without apportionment among the several States, and without regard to any census or enumeration.

Amendment 17 *(Ratified April 8, 1913)*

The Senate of the United States shall be composed of two Senators from each State, elected by the people thereof, for six years; and each Senator shall have one vote. The electors in each State shall have the qualifications requisite for electors of the most numerous branch of the State legislatures.

When vacancies happen in the representation of any State in the Senate, the executive authority of such State shall issue writs of election to fill such vacancies: Provided, That the legislature of any State may empower the executive thereof to make temporary appointments until the people fill the vacancies by election as the legislature may direct.

This amendment shall not be so construed as to affect the election or term of any Senator chosen before it becomes valid as part of the Constitution.

Amendment 18 *(Ratified January 16, 1919)*

Section 1. After one year from the ratification of this article the manufacture, sale, or transportation of intoxicating liquors within, the importation thereof into, or the exportation thereof from the United States and all territory subject to the jurisdiction thereof for beverage purposes is hereby prohibited.

Section 2. The Congress and the several States shall have concurrent power to enforce this article by appropriate legislation.

Section 3. This article shall be inoperative unless it shall have been ratified as an amendment to the Constitution by the legislatures of the several States, as provided in the Constitution, within seven years from the date of the submission hereof to the States by the Congress.

Amendment 19 *(Ratified August 18, 1920)*

The right of citizens of the United States to vote shall not be denied or abridged by the United States or by any State on account of sex.

Congress shall have power to enforce this article by appropriate legislation.

Amendment 20 *(Ratified January 23, 1933)*

Section 1. The terms of the President and Vice President shall end at noon on the 20th day of January, and the terms of Senators and Representatives at noon on the third day of January, of the years in which such terms would have ended if this article had not been ratified; and the terms of their successors shall then begin.

Section 2. The Congress shall assemble at least once in every year, and such meeting shall begin at noon on the third day of January, unless they shall by law appoint a different day.

Section 3. If, at the time fixed for the beginning of the term of the President, the President elect shall have died, the Vice President elect shall become President. If a President shall not have been chosen before the time fixed for the beginning of his term, or if the President elect shall have failed to qualify, then the Vice President elect shall act as President until a President shall have qualified; and the Congress may by law provide for the case wherein neither a President elect nor a Vice President elect shall have qualified, declaring who shall then act as President, or the manner in which one who is to act shall be selected, and such person shall act accordingly until a President or Vice President shall have qualified.

Section 4. The Congress may by law provide for the case of the death of any of the persons from whom the House of Representatives may choose a President whenever the right of choice shall have devolved upon them, and for the case of the death of any of the persons from whom the Senate may choose a Vice President whenever the right of choice shall have devolved upon them.

Section 5. Sections 1 and 2 shall take effect on the 15th day of October following the ratification of this article.

Section 6. This article shall be inoperative unless it shall have been ratified as an amendment to the Constitution by the legislatures of three-fourths of the several States within seven years from the date of its submission.

Amendment 21 *(Ratified December 5, 1933)*
Section 1. The eighteenth article of amendment to the Constitution of the United States is hereby repealed.

Section 2. The transportation or importation into any State, Territory, or possession of the United States for delivery or use therein of intoxicating liquors, in violation of the laws thereof, is hereby prohibited.

Section 3. This article shall be inoperative unless it shall have been ratified as an amendment to the Constitution by conventions in the several States, as provided in the Constitution, within seven years from the date of the submission hereof to the States by the Congress.

Amendment 22 *(Ratified February 27, 1951)*
Section 1. No person shall be elected to the office of the President more than twice, and no person who has held the office of President, or acted as President, for more than two years of a term to which some other person was elected President shall be elected to the office of the President more than once. But this Article shall not apply to any person holding the office of President when this Article was proposed by the Congress, and shall not prevent any person who may be holding the office of President, or acting as President, during the term within which this Article becomes operative from holding the office of President or acting as President during the remainder of such term.

Section 2. This article shall be inoperative unless it shall have been ratified as an amendment to the Constitution by the legislatures of three-fourths of the several States within seven years from the date of its submission to the States by the Congress.

Amendment 23 *(Ratified March 29, 1961)*
Section 1. The District constituting the seat of Government of the United States shall appoint in such manner as the Congress may direct:

A number of electors of President and Vice President equal to the whole number of Senators and Representatives in Congress to which the District would be entitled if it were a State, but in no event more than the least populous State; they shall be in addition to those appointed by the States, but they shall be considered, for the purposes of the election of President and Vice President, to be electors appointed by a State; and they shall meet in the District and perform such duties as provided by the twelfth article of amendment.

Section 2. The Congress shall have power to enforce this article by appropriate legislation.

Amendment 24 *(Ratified January 23, 1964)*
Section 1. The right of citizens of the United States to vote in any primary or other election for President or Vice President, for electors for President or Vice President, or for Senator or Representative in Congress, shall not be denied or abridged by the United States or any State by reason of failure to pay any poll tax or other tax.

Section 2. The Congress shall have power to enforce this article by appropriate legislation.

Amendment 25 *(Ratified February 10, 1967)*
Section 1. In case of the removal of the President from office or of his death or resignation, the Vice President shall become President.

Section 2. Whenever there is a vacancy in the office of the Vice President, the President shall nominate a Vice President who shall take office upon confirmation by a majority vote of both Houses of Congress.

Section 3. Whenever the President transmits to the President *pro tempore* of the Senate and the Speaker of the House of Representatives his written declaration that he is unable to discharge the powers and duties of his office, and until he transmits to them a written declaration to the contrary, such powers and duties shall be discharged by the Vice President as Acting President.

Section 4. Whenever the Vice President and a majority of either the principal officers of the executive departments or of such other body as Congress may by law provide, transmit to the President *pro tempore* of the Senate and the Speaker of the House of Representatives their written declaration that the President is unable to discharge the powers and duties of his office, the Vice President shall immediately assume the powers and duties of the office as Acting President.

Thereafter, when the President transmits to the President *pro tempore* of the Senate and the Speaker of the House of Representatives his written declaration that no inability exists, he shall resume the powers and duties of his office unless the Vice President and a majority of either the principal officers of the executive department or of such other body as Congress may by law provide, transmit within four days to the President *pro tempore* of the Senate and the Speaker of the House of Representatives their written declaration that the President is unable to discharge the powers and duties of his office. Thereupon Congress shall decide the issue, assembling within forty-eight hours for that purpose if not in session. If the Congress, within twenty-one days after receipt of the latter written declaration, or, if Congress is not in session, within twenty-one days after Congress is required to assemble, determines by two-thirds vote of both Houses that the President is unable to discharge the powers and duties of his office, the Vice President shall continue to discharge the same as Acting President; otherwise, the President shall resume the powers and duties of his office.

Amendment 26 *(Ratified July 1, 1971)*
Section 1. The right of citizens of the United States, who are eighteen years of age or older, to vote shall not be denied or abridged by the United States or by any State on account of age.

Section 2. The Congress shall have power to enforce this article by appropriate legislation.

Amendment 27 *(Ratified May 18, 1992)*
No law, varying the compensation for the services of the [United States] Senators and Representatives, shall take effect, until an election of Representatives shall have intervened.

Appendix III

THE
GETTYSBURG
ADDRESS

FOUR SCORE AND SEVEN YEARS AGO our fathers brought forth, upon this continent, a new nation, conceived in Liberty, and dedicated to the proposition that all men are created equal.

Now we are engaged in a great civil war, testing whether that nation, or any nation, so conceived, and so dedicated, can long endure. We are met here on a great battlefield of that war. We have come to dedicate a portion of it as a final resting place for those who here gave their lives that that nation might live. It is altogether fitting and proper that we should do this.

But in a larger sense we can not dedicate—we can not consecrate—we can not hallow this ground. The brave men, living and dead, who struggled here, have consecrated it far above our poor power to add or detract. The world will little note, nor long remember, what we say here, but can never forget what they did here. It is for us, the living, rather to be dedicated here to the unfinished work which they have, thus far, so nobly carried on. It is rather for us to be here dedicated to the great task remaining before us—that from these honored dead we take increased devotion to that cause for which they here gave the last full measure of devotion—that we here highly resolve that these dead shall not have died in vain; that this nation shall have a new birth of freedom; and that this government of the people, by the people, for the people, shall not perish from the earth.

—Abraham Lincoln
November 19, 1863

Appendix IV

LETTER FROM BIRMINGHAM JAIL

April 16, 1963
Birmingham, Alabama

My Dear Fellow Clergymen:

WHILE CONFINED HERE in the Birmingham city jail, I came across your recent statement calling my present activities "unwise and un-timely." Seldom do I pause to answer criticism of my work and ideas. If I sought to answer all the criticisms that cross my desk, my secretaries would have little time for anything other than such correspondence in the course of the day, and I would have no time for constructive work. But since I feel that you are men of genuine good will and that your criticisms are sincerely set forth, I want to try to answer your state-ment in what I hope will be patient and reasonable terms.

I think I should indicate why I am here in Birmingham, since you have been influenced by the view which argues against "outsiders coming in." I have the honor of serving as President of the Southern Christian Leadership Conference, an organization operating in every southern state, with headquarters in Atlanta, Georgia. We have some eighty-five affiliated organizations across the South, and one of them is the Alabama Christian Movement for Human Rights. Frequently we share staff, educational and financial resources with our affiliates. Several months ago the affiliate here in Birmingham asked us to be on call to engage in a nonviolent direct-action program if such were deemed necessary. We readily consented, and when the hour came we lived up to our promise. So I, along with several members of my staff, am here because I was invited here. I am here because I have organizational ties here.

But more basically, I am in Birmingham because injustice is here. Just as the prophets of the eighth century B.C. left their villages and carried their "thus saith the Lord" far beyond the boundaries of their home towns, and just as the Apostle Paul left his village of Tarsus and carried the gospel of Jesus Christ to the far corners of the Greco-Roman world, so am I compelled to carry the gospel of freedom beyond my own home town. Like Paul, I must constantly respond to the Macedonian call for aid.

Moreover, I am cognizant of the interrelatedness of all communities and states. I cannot sit by in Atlanta and not be concerned about what happens in Birmingham. Injustice anywhere is a threat to justice everywhere. We are caught in an inescapable network of mutuality, tied in a single garment of destiny. Whatever affects one directly, affects all indirectly. Never again can we afford to live with the narrow, provincial "outside agitator" idea. Anyone who lives inside the United States can never be considered an outsider anywhere within its bounds.

You deplore the demonstrations taking place in Birmingham. But your statement, I am sorry to say, fails to express a similar concern for the conditions that brought about the demonstrations. I am sure that none of you would want to rest content with the superficial kind of social analysis that deals merely with effects and does not grapple with underlying causes. It is unfortunate that demonstrations are taking place in Birmingham, but it is even more unfortunate that the city's white power structure left the Negro community with no alternative.

In any nonviolent campaign there are four basic steps: collection of the facts to determine whether injustices exist; negotiation; self-purification; and direct action. We have gone through all these steps in Birmingham. There can be no gainsaying the fact that racial injustice engulfs this community. Birmingham is probably the most thoroughly segregated city in the United States. Its ugly record of brutality is widely known. Negroes have experienced grossly unjust treatment in the courts. There have been more unsolved bombings of Negro homes and churches in Birmingham that in any other city in the nation. These are the hard, brutal facts of the case. On the basis of these conditions, Negro leaders sought to negotiate with the city fathers. But the latter consistently refused to engage in good-faith negotiation.

Then, last September, came the opportunity to talk with leaders of Birmingham's economic community. In the course of the negotiations, certain promises were made by the merchants—for example, to remove the stores' humiliating racial signs. On the basis of these promises, the Reverend Fred Shuttlesworth and the leaders of the Alabama Christian Movement for Human Rights agreed to a moratorium on all demonstrations. As the weeks and months went by, we realized that we were the victims of a broken promise. A few signs, briefly removed, returned; the others remained.

As in so may past experiences, our hopes had been blasted, and the shadow of deep disappointment settled upon us. We had no alternative except to prepare for direct action, whereby we would present our very bodies as a means of laying our case before the conscience of the local and the national community. Mindful of the difficulties involved, we decided to undertake a process of self-purification. We began a series of workshops on nonviolence, and we repeatedly asked ourselves: "Are you able to accept blows without retaliation?" "Are you able to endure the ordeal of jail?" We decided to schedule our direct-action program for the Easter season, realizing that except for Christmas, this is the main shopping period of the year. Knowing that a strong economic-withdrawal program would be the byproduct of direct action, we felt that this would be the best time to bring pressure to bear on the merchants for the needed change.

Then it occurred to us that Birmingham's mayoralty election was coming up in March, and we speedily decided to postpone action until after election day. When we discovered that the Commissioner of Public Safety, Eugene "Bull" Connor, had piled up enough votes to be in the run-off, we decided again to postpone action until the day after the run-off so that the demonstrations could not be used to cloud the issues. Like many others, we waited to see Mr. Connor defeated, and to this end we endured postponement after postponement. Having aided in this community need, we felt that our direct-action program could be delayed no longer.

You may well ask: "Why direct action? Why sit-ins, marches, and so forth? Isn't negotiation a better path?" You are quite right in calling for negotiation. Indeed, this is the very purpose of direct action. Nonviolent direct action seeks to create such a crisis and foster such a tension that a community which has constantly refused to negotiate is forced to confront the issue. It seeks so to dramatize the issue that it can no longer be ignored. My citing the creation of tension as part of the work of the nonviolent resister may sound rather shocking. But I must confess that I am not afraid of the word "tension." I have earnestly opposed violent tension, but there is a type of constructive, nonviolent tension which is necessary for growth. Just as Socrates felt that it was necessary to create a tension in the mind so that individuals could rise from the bondage of myths and half-truths to the unfettered realm of creative analysis and objective appraisal, so must we see the need for nonviolent gadflies to create the kind of tension in society that will help men rise from the dark depths of prejudice and racism to the majestic heights of understanding and brotherhood.

The purpose of our direct-action program is to create a situation so crisis-packed that it will inevitably open the door to negotiation, I therefore concur with you in your call for negotiation. Too long has our beloved Southland been bogged down in a tragic effort to live in monologue rather than dialogue.

One of the basic points in your statement is that the action that I and my associates have taken in Birmingham is untimely. Some have asked: "Why didn't you give the new city administration time to act?" The only answer that I can give to this query is that the new Birmingham administration must be prodded about as much as the outgoing one, before it will act. We are sadly mistaken if we feel that the election of Albert Boutwell as mayor will bring the millennium to Birmingham. While Mr. Boutwell is a much more gentle person that Mr. Connor, they are both segregationists, dedicated to maintenance of the status quo. I have hoped that Mr. Boutwell will be reasonable enough to see the futility of massive resistance to desegregation. But he will not see this without pressure from devotees of civil rights. My friends, I must say to you that we have not made a single gain in civil rights without determined legal and nonviolent pressure. Lamentably, it is an historical fact that privileged groups seldom give up their privileges voluntarily. Individuals may see the moral light and voluntarily give up their unjust posture; but as Reinhold Niebuhr has reminded us, groups tend to be more immoral than individuals.

We know through painful experience that freedom is never voluntarily given by the oppressor; it must be demanded by the oppressed. Frankly, I have yet to engage in a direct-action campaign that was "well timed" in the view of those who have not suffered unduly from the disease of segregation. For years now I have heard the word "wait!" It rings in the ear of every Negro with piercing familiarity. This "Wait" has almost always meant "Never." We must come to see, with one of our distinguished jurists, that "justice too long delayed is justice denied."

We have waited for more than 340 years for our constitutional and God-given rights. The nations of Asia and Africa are moving with jetlike speed toward gaining political independence, but we still creep at horse-and-buggy pace toward gaining a cup of coffee at a lunch counter. Perhaps it is easy for those who have never felt the stinging darts of segregation to say, "Wait." But when you have seen vicious mobs lynch your mothers and fathers at will and drown your sisters and brothers at whim; when you have seen hate-filled policemen curse, kick, and even kill your black brothers and sisters; when you see the vast majority of your twenty million Negro brothers smothering in an airtight cage of poverty in the midst of an affluent society; when you suddenly find your tongue twisted and your speech stammering as you seek to explain to your six-year-old daughter why she can't go to the public amusement park that has just been advertised on television, and see tears welling up in her eyes when she is told that Funtown is closed to colored children, and see ominous clouds of inferiority beginning to form in her little mental sky, and see her beginning to distort her personality by developing an unconscious bitterness toward white people; when you have to concoct an answer for a five-year-old son who is asking, "Daddy, why do white people treat colored people so mean?"; when you take a cross-country drive and find it necessary to sleep night after night in the uncomfortable corners of your automobile because no motel will accept you; when you are humiliated day in and day out by nagging signs reading "white" and "colored"; when your first name becomes "Nigger," your middle name becomes "boy" (however old you are) and your last name becomes "John," and your wife and mother are never given the respected title "Mrs."; when you are harried by day and haunted by night by the fact that you are a Negro, living constantly at tiptoe stance, never quite knowing what to expect next, and are plagued with inner fears and outer resentments; when you are forever fighting a degenerating sense of "nobodiness"— then you will understand why we find it difficult to wait. There comes a time when the cup of endurance runs over, and men are no longer willing to be plunged into the abyss of despair. I hope, sirs, you can understand our legitimate and unavoidable impatience.

You express a great deal of anxiety over our willingness to break laws. This is certainly a legitimate concern. Since we so diligently urge people to obey the Supreme Court's decision of 1954 outlawing segregation in the public schools, at first glance it may seem rather paradoxical for us consciously to break laws. One may ask: "How can you advocate breaking some laws and obeying others?" The answer lies in the fact that there are two types of laws: just and unjust. I would be the first to advocate obeying just laws. One has not only a legal but a moral responsibility to obey just laws. Conversely, one has a moral responsibility to disobey unjust laws. I would agree with St. Augustine that "an unjust law is no law at all."

Now, what is the difference between the two? How does one determine whether a law is just or unjust? A just law is a manmade code that squares with the moral law or the law of God. An unjust law is a code that is out of Harmony with the moral law. To put it in the terms of St. Thomas Aquinas: An unjust law is a human law that is not rooted in eternal law and natural law. Any law that uplifts human personality is just. Any law that degrades human personality is unjust. All segregation statutes are unjust because segregation distorts the soul and damages the personality. It gives the segregator a false sense of superiority and the segregated a false sense of inferiority. Segregation, to use the terminology of the Jewish philosopher Martin Buber, substitutes an "I-it" relationship for an "I-thou" relationship and ends up relegating persons to the status of things. Hence segregation is not only politically, economically and sociologically unsound, it is morally wrong and sinful. Paul Tillich has said that sin is separation. Is not segregation an existential expression of man's tragic separation, his awful estrangement, his terrible sinfulness? Thus is it that I can urge men to obey the 1954 decision of the Supreme Court, for it is morally right; and I can urge them to disobey segregation ordinances, for they are morally wrong.

Let us consider a more concrete example of just and unjust laws. An unjust law is a code that a numerical or power majority group compels a minority group to obey but does not make binding on itself. This is *difference* made legal. By the same token, a just law is a code that a majority compels a minority to follow and that it is willing to follow itself. This is *sameness* made legal.

Let me give another explanation. A law is unjust if it is inflicted on a minority that, as a result of being denied the right to vote, had no part in enacting or devising the law. Who can say that the legislature of Alabama which set up that state's segregation laws was democratically elected? Throughout Alabama all sorts of devious methods are used to prevent Negroes from becoming registered voters, and there are some counties in which, even though Negroes constitute a majority of the population, not a single Negro is registered. Can any law enacted under such circumstances be considered democratically structured?

Sometimes a law is just on its face and unjust in its application. For instance, I have been arrested on a charge of parading without a permit. Now, there is nothing wrong in having an ordinance which requires a permit for a parade. But such an ordinance becomes unjust when it is used to maintain segregation and to deny citizens the First Amendment privilege of peaceful assembly and protest.

I hope you are able to see the distinction I am trying to point out. In no sense do I advocate evading or defying the law, as would the rabid segregationist. That would lead to anarchy. One who breaks an unjust law must do so openly, lovingly, and with a willingness to accept the penalty. I submit that an individual who breaks a law that conscience tells him is unjust, and who willingly accepts the penalty of imprisonment in order to arouse the conscience of the community over its injustice, is in reality expressing the highest respect for law.

Of course, there is nothing new about this kind of civil disobedience. It was evidenced sublimely in the refusal of Shadrach, Meshach, and Abednego to obey the laws of Nebuchadnezzar, on the ground that a higher moral law was at stake. It was practiced superbly by the early Christians, who were willing to face hungry lions and the excruciating pain of chopping blocks rather than submit to certain unjust laws of the Roman Empire. To a degree, academic freedom is a reality today because Socrates practiced civil disobedience. In our own nation, the Boston Tea Party represented a massive act of civil disobedience.

We should never forget that everything Adolf Hitler did in Germany was "legal" and everything the Hungarian freedom fighters did in Hungary was "illegal." It was "illegal" to aid and comfort a Jew in Hitler's Germany. Even so, I am sure that, had I lived in Germany at the time, I would have aided and comforted my Jewish brothers. If today I lived in a Communist country where certain principles dear to the Christian faith are suppressed, I would openly advocate disobeying that country's antireligious laws.

I must make two honest confessions to you, my Christian and Jewish brothers. First, I must confess that over the past few years I have been gravely disappointed with the white moderate. I have almost reached the regrettable conclusion that the Negro's great stumbling block in his stride toward freedom is not the White Citizen's Councilor or the Ku Klux Klanner, but the white moderate, who is more devoted to "order" than to justice; who prefers a negative peace which is the absence of tension to a positive peace which is the presence of justice; who constantly says, "I agree with you in the goal you seek, but I cannot agree with your methods of direct action"; who paternalistically believes he can set the timetable for another man's freedom; who lives by a mythical concept of time and who constantly advises the Negro the wait for a "more convenient season." Shallow understanding from people of good will is more frustrating than absolute understanding from people of ill will. Lukewarm acceptance is much more bewildering than outright rejection.

I had hoped that the white moderate would understand that law and order exist for the purpose of establishing justice and that when they fail in this purpose they become the dangerously structured dams that block the flow of social progress. I had hoped that the white moderate would understand that the present tension in the South is a necessary phase of the transition from an obnoxious negative peace, in which the Negro passively accepted his unjust plight, to a substantive and positive peace, in which all men will respect the dignity and worth of human personality. Actually, we who engage in nonviolent direct action are not the creators of tension. We merely bring to the surface the hidden tension that is already alive. We bring it out in the open, where it can be seen and dealt with. Like a boil that can never be cured so long as it is covered up but must be opened with all its ugliness to the natural medicines of air and light, injustice must be exposed with all the tension its exposure creates, to the light of human conscience and the air of national opinion, before it can be cured.

In your statement you assert that our actions, even though peaceful, must be condemned because they precipitate violence. But is this a logical assertion? Isn't this like condemning a robbed man because his possession of money precipitated the evil act of robbery? Isn't this like condemning Socrates because his unswerving commitment to truth and his philosophical inquiries precipitated the act by the misguided populace in which they made him drink hemlock? Isn't this like condemning Jesus because his unique God-consciousness and never-ceasing devotion to God's will precipitated the evil act of cruci-fixion? We must come to see that, as the federal courts have consis-tently affirmed, it is wrong to urge an individual to cease his efforts to gain his basic constitutional rights because the quest may precipitate violence. Society must protect the robbed and punish the robber.

I had also hoped that the white moderate would reject the myth concerning time in relation to the struggle for freedom. I have just received a letter from a white brother in Texas. He writes "All Chris-tians know that the colored people will receive equal rights eventu-ally, but it is possible that you are in too great a religious hurry. It has taken Christianity almost two thousand years to accomplish what it has. The teachings of Christ take time to come to earth." Such an attitude stems from a tragic misconception of time, from the strangely irrational notion that there is something in the very flow of time that will inevitably cure all ills. Actually, time itself is neutral; it can be used either destructively or constructively. More and more I feel that the people of ill will have used time much more effectively than have the people of good will. We will have to repent in the generation not merely for the hateful words and actions of the bad people, but for the appalling silence of the good people. Human progress never rolls in on wheels of inevitability; it comes through the tireless efforts of men willing to be co-workers with God, and without this hard work, time itself becomes an ally of the forces of stagnation. We must use time creatively, in the knowledge that the time is always ripe to do right. Now is the time to make real the promise of democracy and trans-form our pending national elegy into a creative psalm of brother-hood. Now is the time to lift our national policy from the quicksand of racial injustice to the solid rock of human dignity.

You speak of our activity in Birmingham as extreme. At first I was rather disappointed that fellow clergymen would see my nonvio-lent efforts as those of an extremist. I began thinking about the fact that I stand in the middle of two opposing forces in the Negro com-munity. One is a force of complacency, made up in part of Negroes who, as a result of long years of oppression, are so drained of self-respect and a sense of "somebodiness" that they have adjusted to segregation; and in part of a few middle-class Negroes who, because of a degree of academic and economic security and because in some ways they profit by segregation, have become insensitive to the problems of the masses. The other force is one of bitterness and hatred, and it comes perilously close to advocating violence. It is expressed in the various black nationalist groups that are springing up across the nation, the largest and best-known being Elijah Muhammad's Muslim movement. Nourished by the Negro's frustration over the continued existence of racial discrimination, this movement is made up of people who have lost faith in America, who have absolutely repudiated Christianity, and who have concluded that the white man is an incorrigible "devil."

I have tried to stand between these two forces, saying that we need emulate neither the "do-nothingism" of the complacent nor the hatred and despair of the black nationalist. For there is the more excellent way of love and nonviolent protest. I am grateful to God that, through the influence of the Negro church, the way of nonviolence became an integral part of our struggle.

If this philosophy had not emerged, by now many streets of the South would, I am convinced, be flowing with blood. And I am further convinced that if our white brothers dismiss as "rabble-rousers" and "outside agitators" those of us who employ nonviolent direct action, and if they refuse to support our nonviolent efforts, millions of Negroes will, out of frustration and despair, seek solace and security in black-nationalist ideologies—a development that would inevitably lead to a frightening racial nightmare.

Oppressed people cannot remain oppressed forever. The yearning for freedom eventually manifests itself, and that is what has happened to the American Negro. Something within has reminded him of his birthright of freedom, and something without has reminded him that it can be gained. Consciously or unconsciously, he has been caught up by the Zeitgeist, and with his black brothers of Africa and his brown and yellow brothers of Asia, South America, and the Caribbean, the United States Negro is moving with a sense of great urgency toward the promised land of racial justice. If one recognizes this vital urge that has engulfed the Negro community, one should readily understand why public demonstrations are taking place. The Negro has many pent-up resentments and latent frustrations, and he must release them. So let him march; let him make prayer pilgrimages to the city hall; let him go on freedom rides—and try to understand why he must do so. If his repressed emotions are not released in nonviolent ways, they will seek expression through violence; this is not a threat but a fact of history. So I have not said to my people, "Get rid of your discontent." Rather, I have tried to say that this normal and healthy discontent can be channeled into the creative outlet of nonviolent direct action. And now this approach is being termed extremist.

But though I was initially disappointed at being categorized as an extremist, as I continued to think about the matter I gradually gained a measure of satisfaction from the label. Was not Jesus an extremist for love: "Love your enemies, bless them that curse you, do good to them that hate you, and pray for them which despitefully use you, and persecute you." Was not Amos an extremist for justice: "Let justice roll down like waters and righteousness like an ever-flowing stream." Was not Paul an extremist for the Christian gospel: "I bear in my body the marks of the Lord Jesus." Was not Martin Luther an extremist: "Here I stand; I cannot do otherwise, so help me God." And John Bunyan: "I will stay in jail to the end of my days before I make a butchery of my conscience." And Abraham Lincoln: "This nation cannot survive half slave and half free." And Thomas Jefferson: "We hold these truths to be self-evident, that all men are created equal ..." So the question is not whether we will be extremists, but what kind of extremists we will be. Will we be extremists for hate or for love? Will we be extremists for the preservation of injustice or for the extension of justice? In that dramatic scene on Calvary's hill three men were crucified. We must never forget that all three were crucified for the same crime—the crime of extremism. Two were extremists for immorality, and thus fell below their environment. The other, Jesus Christ, was an extremist for love, truth, and goodness, and thereby rose above his environment. Perhaps the South, the nation, and the world are in dire need of creative extremists.

I had hoped that the white moderate would see this need. Perhaps I was too optimistic; perhaps I expected too much. I suppose I should have realized that few members of the oppressor race can understand the deep groans and passionate yearnings of the oppressed race, and still fewer have the vision to see that injustice must be rooted out by strong, persistent, and determined action. I am thankful, however, that some of our white brothers in the South have grasped the meaning of this social revolution and committed themselves to it. They are still all too few in quantity, but they are big in quality. Some—such as Ralph McGill, Lillian Smith, Harry Golden, James McBride Dabbs, Ann Braden, and Sarah Patton Boyle—have written about our struggle in eloquent and prophetic terms. Others have marched with us down nameless streets of the South. They have languished in filthy, roach-infested jails, suffering the abuse and brutality of policemen who view them as "dirty nigger-lovers." Unlike many of their moderate brothers and sisters, they have recognized the urgency of the moment and sensed the need for powerful "action" antidotes to combat the disease of segregation.

Let me take note of my other major disappointment. I have been so greatly disappointed with the white church and its leadership. Of course, there are some notable exceptions. I am not unmindful of the fact that each of you has taken some significant stands on this issue. I commend you, Reverend Stallings, for your Christian stand on this past Sunday, in welcoming Negroes to your worship service on a nonsegregated basis. I commend the Catholic leaders of this state for integrating Spring Hill College several years ago.

But despite these notable exceptions, I must honestly reiterate that I have been disappointed with the church. I say this as a minister of the gospel, who loves the church; who was nurtured in its bosom; who has been sustained by its spiritual blessings and who will remain true to it as long as the cord of life shall lengthen.

When I was suddenly catapulted into the leadership of the bus protest in Montgomery, Alabama, a few years ago, I felt we would be supported by the white church. I felt that the ministers, priests, and rabbis of the South would be among our strongest allies. Instead, some have been outright opponents, refusing to understand the freedom movement and misrepresenting its leaders; all too many others have been more cautious than courageous and have remained silent behind the anesthetizing security of stained-glass windows.

In spite of my shattered dreams, I came to Birmingham with the hope that the white religious leadership of this community would see the justice of our cause and, with deep moral concern, would serve as the channel through which our just grievances could reach the power structure. I had hoped that each of you would understand. But again I have been disappointed.

I have heard numerous southern religious leaders admonish their worshipers to comply with a desegregation decision because it is the law, but I have longed to hear white ministers declare: "Follow this decree because integration is morally right and because the Negro is your brother." In the midst of blatant injustices inflicted upon the Negro, I have watched white churchmen stand on the sideline and mouth pious irrelevancies and sanctimonious trivialities. In the midst of a mighty struggle to rid our nation of racial and economic injustice, I have heard many ministers say: "Those are social issues, with which the gospel has no real concern." And I have watched many churches commit themselves to a completely otherworldly religion which makes a strange un-Biblical distinction between body and soul, between the sacred and the secular.

I have traveled the length and breadth of Alabama, Mississippi, and all the other southern states. On sweltering summer days and crisp autumn mornings I have looked at the South's beautiful churches with their lofty spires pointing heavenward. I have beheld the impressive outlines of her massive religious-education buildings. Over and over I have found myself asking: What kind of people worship here? Who is their God? Where were their voices when the lips of Governor Barnett dripped with words of interposition and nullification? Where were they when Governor Wallace gave a clarion call of defiance and hatred? Where were their voices of support when bruised and weary Negro men and women decided to rise from the dark dungeons of complacency to the bright hills of creative protest?"

Yes, these questions are still in my mind. In deep disappointment I have wept over the laxity of the church. But be assured that my tears have been tears of love. Yes, I love the church. How could I do otherwise? I am in the rather unique position of being the son, the grandson, and the great-grandson of preachers. Yes, I see the church as the body of Christ. But, oh! How we have blemished and scarred that body through social neglect and through fear of being nonconformists.

There was a time when the church was very powerful—in the time when the early Christians rejoiced at being deemed worthy to suffer for what they believed. In those days the church was not merely a thermometer that recorded the ideas and principles of popular opinion; it was a thermostat that transformed the mores of society. Whenever the early Christians entered a town, the people in power became disturbed and immediately sought to convict the Christians for being "disturbers of the peace" and "outside agitators." But the Christians pressed on, in the conviction that they were "a colony of heaven," called to obey God rather than man. Small in number, they were big in commitment. They were too God-intoxicated to be "astronomically intimidated." By their effort and example they brought an end to such ancient evils as infanticide and gladiatorial contests.

Things are different now. So often the contemporary church is a weak, ineffectual voice with an uncertain sound. So often it is an arch-defender of the status quo. Far from being disturbed by the presence of the church, the power structure of the average community is consoled by the church's silent—and often even vocal—sanction of things as they are. But the judgment of God is upon the church as never before. If today's church does not recapture the sacrificial spirit of the early church, it will lose its authenticity, forfeit the loyalty of millions, and be dismissed as an irrelevant social club with no meaning for the twentieth century. Every day I meet young people whose disappointment with the church has turned into outright disgust.

Perhaps I have once again been too optimistic. Is organized religion too inextricably bound to the status quo to save our nation and the world? Perhaps I must turn my faith to the inner spiritual church, the church within the church, as the true *ekklesia* and the hope of the world. But again I am thankful to God that some noble souls from the ranks of organized religion have broken loose from the paralyzing chains of conformity and joined us as active partners in the struggle for freedom. They have left their secure congregations and walked the streets of Albany, Georgia, with us. They have gone down the highways of the South on tortuous rides for freedom. Yes, they have gone to jail with us. Some have been dismissed from their churches, have lost the support of their bishops and fellow ministers. But they have acted in the faith that right defeated is stronger than evil triumphant. Their witness has been the spiritual salt that has preserved the true meaning of the gospel in these troubled times. They have carved a tunnel of hope through the dark mountain of disappointment.

I hope the church as a whole will meet the challenge of this decisive hour. But even if the church does not come to the aid of justice, I have no despair about the future. I have no fear about the outcome of our struggle in Birmingham, even if our motives are at present misunderstood. We will reach the goal of freedom in Birmingham and all over the nation, because the goal of America is freedom. Abused and scorned though we may be, our destiny is tied up with America's destiny. Before the pilgrims landed at Plymouth, we were here. For more than two centuries our forebears labored in this country without wages; they made cotton king; they built the homes of their masters while suffering gross injustice and shameful humiliation—and yet out of bottomless vitality they continued to thrive and develop. If the inexpressible cruelties of slavery could not stop us, the opposition we now face will surely fail. We will win our freedom because the sacred heritage of our nation and the eternal will of God are embodied in our echoing demands.

Before closing I feel impelled to mention one other point in your statement that has troubled me profoundly. You warmly commended the Birmingham police force for keeping "order" and "preventing violence." I doubt that you would so quickly commend the policemen if you were to observe their ugly and inhumane treatment of Negroes here in the city jail; if you were to watch them push and curse old Negro women and young Negro girls; if you were to see them slap and kick Negro men and young boys; if you were to observe them, as they did on two occasions, refuse to give us food because we wanted to sing our grace together. I cannot join you in your praise of the Birmingham police department.

It is true that the police have exercised a degree of discipline in handling the demonstrations. In this sense they have conducted themselves rather "nonviolently" in public. But for what purpose? To preserve the evil system of segregation. Over the past few years I have consistently preached that nonviolence demands that the means we use must be as pure as the ends we seek. I have tried to make clear that it is wrong to use immoral means to attain moral ends. But now I must affirm that it is just as wrong, or perhaps even more so, to use moral means to preserve immoral ends. Perhaps Mr. Connor and his policemen have been rather nonviolent in public, as was Chief Pritchett in Albany, Georgia, but they have used the moral means of nonviolence to maintain the immoral end of racial injustice. As T. S. Eliot has said, "The last temptation is the greatest treason: To do the right deed for the wrong reason."

I wish you had commended the Negro sit-inners and demonstrators of Birmingham for their sublime courage, their willingness to suffer, and their amazing discipline in the midst of great provocation. One day the South will recognize its real heroes. They will be the James Merediths, with the noble sense of purpose that enables them to face jeering and hostile mobs, and with the agonizing loneliness that characterizes the life of the pioneer. They will be old, oppressed, battered Negro women, symbolized in a seventy-two-year-old woman in Montgomery, Alabama, who rose up with a sense of dignity and when her people decided not to ride segregated buses, who responded with ungrammatical profundity to one who inquired about her weariness: "My feets is tired, but my soul is at rest." They will be the young high school and college students, the young ministers of the gospel and a host of their elders, courageously and nonviolently sitting in at lunch counters and willingly going to jail for conscience's sake. One day the South will know that when these disinherited children of God sat down at lunch counters, they were in reality standing up for what is best in the American Dream and for the most sacred values in our Judaeo-Christian heritage, thereby bringing our nation back to those great wells of democracy which were dug deep by the founding fathers in their formulation of the Constitution and the Declaration of Independence.

Never before have I written so long a letter. I'm afraid it is much too long to take your precious time. I can assure you that it would have been much shorter if I had been writing from a comfortable desk, but what else can one do when he is alone in a narrow jail cell, other than write long letters, think long thoughts, and pray long prayers?

If I have said anything in this letter that overstates the truth and indicates an unreasonable impatience, I beg you to forgive me. If I have said anything that understates the truth and indicates my having a patience that allows me to settle for anything less than brotherhood, I beg God to forgive me.

I hope this letter finds you strong in the faith. I also hope that circumstances will soon make it possible for me to meet each of you, not as an integrationist or a civil-rights leader but as a fellow clergyman and a Christian brother. Let us all hope that the dark clouds of racial prejudice will soon pass away and the deep fog of misunderstanding will be lifted from our fear-drenched communities, and in some not too distant tomorrow the radiant stars of love and brotherhood will shine over our great nation with all their scintillating beauty.

Yours for the cause of Peace and Brotherhood,

Martin Luther King, Jr.

INDEX

abortion, 59–60
Age of Reason, 58
Aidid (General), 20
Air Force, 44
Alabama, 12
Alaska, 39
Alaska State Council
    for the Arts, 44, 50
American Family Association, 46
American Rangers, 22
American Revolution, 9, 56
anarchy, 10
Anchorage, 39, 40, 43, 48, 49, 50
Anchorage Daily News, 40
Anchorage Times, 40
Angelou, Maya, ix
Aristotle, 29
Army Rangers, 20
Art Institute of Chicago, 40
Articles of Confederation, 4
arts, 39–44, 48–50, 77–78
Asian, 25
Athens, 8

Beatles, The, 39
Becker, Carol, 48
Bentham, Jeremy, 23

Benton, Thomas Hart, 38
Bill of Rights, viii, 6
Birmingham, Ala., 71
Black, Hugo, 54
Boccaccio, 35
Bosnia, 58
Botticelli, 35
Bowdler, Thomas, 37
Bowerman, Bill, 9
Brahms, Johannes, 67
Brandeis, William, 27–28, 29
Brogan, Robin, 43, 51
Bush, George, 15, 40, 77, 78

California, 28
Cambodia, 25
Carr, Perry, 40
censo, 38, 46–47
censorship, x, 35, 38, 45, 46, 47,
    50, 51
character, 14
Chicago, Ill., 39
Christ, 36–37
Christian, 56, 58, 62
Christian Coalition, 63
Church of San Giovanni e Paolo,
    35

Churchill, Winston, 13
Civil War, 60, 70
Clash, The, 1, 25-26
Clinton, Bill, 9, 15
Commager, Henry Steele, 47
common good, viii, 13, 67, 72
Communist Party, 28
compassion, 13, 78
Comstock, Anthony, 37-38, 47
Confucius, 16
Congressional Medal of Honor, 22
conscience, ix, x, 16, 23, 27, 59, 61, 62, 67, 78
conscientious objection, 59
Constitution, U.S., viii, 2, 3, 4-7, 8, 9, 10, 13, 14, 27, 44, 62
Council of Trent, 35

death penalty, 59
Declaration of Independence, The, viii-x, 2, 3, 4-5, 8, 9, 10, 13, 24, 25, 26, 27, 29, 62, 71, 72-73
democracy, x, 9, 11, 15, 48, 49, 54, 58, 67, 72, 73
Descartes, René, 2
"Diabolus in Musica", 38
divine Providence, 3
Dole, Bob, 9
Dos Passos, John, 69-70
Douglas, William O., 49

Einstein, Albert, 13
Emerson, Ralph Waldo, 68
Engel v. Vitale, 53, 54
England, 24

Enlightenment, The, 2, 3, 4, 47
Episcopal Church, 56
Erickson, Jan, 41, 49-50
evil, 22, 28, 46, 58

Feast in the House of Levi, The, 37
Federalist Papers, The, 6, 67, 69
Fink, Tom, 50
Finley, Karen, 39
First Amendment, vii, viii, x, 2, 6, 7, 10, 12, 27, 29, 34, 35, 40, 44, 45, 46, 47, 48, 51, 54, 59, 61, 62, 63, 72-73, 77, 78
First Principles, ix, 24, 26-27, 61, 67, 69, 73
flag, U.S., 40-44
Flag Day, 44
Ford, Henry, 13
Fordice, Kirk, 62
Founding Fathers, 56, 70, 72-73
Fourteenth Amendment, 62
France, 24
Freedom Forum First Amendment Center, The, 78
Freud, Sigmund, 23
Frost, Robert, 68

Germans, 36, 37
Germany, 36-37, 58
Gettysburg Address, The, x, 68, 69-70
Ghirlandaio, 35
Gibbon, Edward, 30
God, 2, 23, 62, 63, 71
Good Samaritan, 22
Grady, Ken, 34

Grant, Ulysses S., 38
Grenada, 25

Hamilton, Alexander, 6
Hand, Learned, 14
Hazo, Samuel, 74
Helms, Jesse, 37, 47
Hillel (Rabbi), 49
Hoffer, Eric, 71
Holmes, Oliver Wendell, 27-28, 29
Hopi, 23
Hughes, Holly, 39
Hume, David, 23
humor, 13

Idaho, 12
"Il Braghettone", 35
"In God We Trust", 62
Indians (Native Americans), 3, 25, 61
Ingram, Jann, 40
Inquisition, The, 37
International Purity Congress, 38
intuition, 12
Iran, 58

James, William, 1
Jay, John, 6
Jefferson, Thomas, 21, 55, 61, 63, 70, 72

Kennedy, John, 11
Khomeni (The Ayatollah), 35
King, Martin Luther Jr., 15, 26, 61, 68, 70, 71, 73
King George III, 2, 71
Ku Klux Klan, 40, 47

language, viii, 6, 67, 68, 78
Lapham, Lewis, 11
"Last Supper, The", 35, 36, 37
laws, 2-7, 9, 10, 22, 27, 28, 56-57, 61, 71-72
leadership, 12-14
Letter from Birmingham Jail, x, 26, 68, 70-72
liberty, vii, ix, x, 3, 10, 24, 25, 28, 29, 60, 61, 69, 70, 71, 73-74
Limbaugh, Rush, 9
Lincoln, Abraham, x, 68, 70, 72
Locke, John, 2
Los Angeles Times, The, 67
Lower, Kriste, 46
Luke, 37

Madison, James, 6, 55, 56, 57, 63, 67, 69, 72
Mannheim, Germany, 37
Mapplethorpe, Robert, 39, 40, 45, 46
Marbury v. Madison, 5
Marshall, John, 5
Mason, James, 57
Massachusetts, 12
McCarthy, Joe, 61
Medici, The, 35
Memorial and Remonstrance Against Religious Assessments, 56
Metropolitan Opera, 38
Michelangelo, 35
Mill, John Stuart, 23
Miller v. California, 7
Mogadishu, 20, 22

morality, 9, 15, 21, 22, 28, 59, 72
Morley, Thomas, 38
Morrison, Toni, 68
Moyers, Bill, 9
music, 38, 39, 67, 68, 77

nation, 1, 6, 14, 24, 29, 37, 56, 60, 69, 72
National Endowment for the Arts, 77
Nazis, 40, 46, 47
Negroes, 25
New York City, 70
New York Times, The, 20
Niebuhr, Reinhold, 58
Nineteenth Amendment, 25
Nixon, Richard, 15
Nobel Prize, 68
North Carolina, 37
Northern Ireland, 58

obscenity, 7, 46, 49, 78
Oregon, 7
Ovid, 35

Paine, Thomas, 9, 57
Palmer, Susan E., 43
Panama, 25
Pennsylvania Supreme Court, 21
Percy, Walker, 11
Perot, Ross, 15
"Persephone", 38
Pfitzenmeier, Robert, 43
Piffle (Archbishop), 38
Pledge of Allegiance, 62
politicians, vii, x, 8, 14, 38, 40, 78,

politicsx, 2-4, 6-7, 8, 14-16, 25, 48, 57-58, 72, 78
prayer, x, 24, 53, 54, 55, 57, 63
Presley, Elvis, 39
press, 5, 28-29, 39, 77
Protestants, 36
public service, 11

rap, 39, 68
reason, 2, 4, 10-11, 14, 42, 46, 58
religion, viii, ix, x, 5, 22-23, 27, 40, 53, 54, 55, 56, 57, 58, 60, 61, 63, 73
Renaissance, 35
Republican, 62
responsibility, vii-x, 7-10, 21, 30, 67, 69-70, 72-74
rights, ix, 1-7, 8-9, 24-27, 37, 43-44, 47, 57, 70-71
Robertson, Pat, 9
Roe v. Wade, 60
Rome, 37
Rushdie, Salman, 35
Russell, Bertrand, 48

Saint John, 37
Saint Peter, 37
Salome, 38
Sartre, Jean-Paul, 23
Satanic Verses, The, 35
Savonarola, Girolamo, 35
Schlafly, Phyllis, 60
Scott, Dread, 40-43
Serrano, Andres, 39
Shakespeare, William, 37

Shaw, George Bernard, vii
Siebels, Ron, 43
Sims, Alice, 40
sin, 23, 56
Sistine Chapel, 35
Socrates, 35
Somalia, 20
Soviet Union, 11
Spain, 24
speech, viii-x, 5, 9, 25-26, 34, 40, 44, 45, 46-47, 48-50, 67-68, 73, 78
speech codes, 24
St. Augustine, 23
Stanford, Verne, 50
Stern, Howard, 9
stewardship, ix, 23
Strauss, Richard, 38
Supreme Court, 4, 7, 42, 49, 53, 60, 63
"Susanna and the Elders", 38

television, vii-viii, 24, 55, 68
Tertullian, 99
Thoreau, Henry David, 68
Tine, Robert, 35
Tocqueville, Alexis de, 58, 59
trust, vii, 13, 15, 61
truth, 15, 29, 42, 49, 56-57, 68, 78
Twain, Mark, 23
tyranny, 2, 11, 13, 58

United Nations, 20
U.S. Department of Labor, 7

VFW, 41
values, ix, 39, 43-44, 54, 57-58, 66-67, 78
Vanderbilt University, 60, 76
Venus de Milo (Aphrodite), 37
Veronese, 35, 36, 37
Vienna, 38, 67
Vietnam, 43, 45
violence, viii, 24, 45
Virginia, 57
Virginia Declaration of Rights, 57
Virginia Legislature, 56
Visual Arts Center (VAC), 39, 40, 41, 43, 44, 50, 51
Volterra, Daniel da, 35

"wall of separation", 55
war, 21-22, 39, 47, 58, 59, 69-70
Washington, D.C., ix, 14, 69, 70
"Water Babies", 40
Weddington, Sara, 60
Welch, Gay, 60
West Side Story, 38
West Virginia, 12
Whitman, Walt, 68
Whitney v. California, 27-28
Williams, Roger, 2
Wilson, Woodrow, 38
World War II, 13, 61

Yania v. Bigan, 21, 31

About the Author

John Frohnmayer is a noted speaker, writer, ethicist and legal scholar. He served as chairman of the National Endowment for the Arts from 1989 to 1992. His first book, *Leaving Town Alive,* describes these turbulent years.

His academic degrees are in American History (Stanford, 1964), Christian Ethics (University of Chicago, 1969) and Law (University of Oregon, 1972). He and his wife, Leah, live in Bozeman, Montana, where he practices law, writes and teaches.